Killer
Interviews

Killer Interviews

Frederick W. Ball
Barbara B. Ball

McGraw-Hill

New York   San Francisco   Washington, D.C.   Auckland   Bogotá
Caracas   Lisbon   London   Madrid   Mexico City   Milan
Montreal   New Delhi   San Juan   Singapore
Sydney   Tokyo   Toronto

Library of Congress Cataloging-in-Publication Data

Ball, Frederick W.
   Killer interviews / Frederick W. Ball, Barbara B. Ball.
      p.   cm.
   Includes index.
   ISBN 0-07-005756-7 (pbk.)
    1. Employment interviewing.   I. Ball, Barbara B.   II Title.
   HF5549.5.I6B333   1996
   650.14—dc20   96-20335
                                                           CIP

McGraw-Hill

A Division of The **McGraw·Hill** *Companies*

7 8 9 0   DOC/DOC 9 0 1 0 9 8

ISBN 0-07-005756-7

*The sponsoring editor for this book was Betsy Brown, the editing
supervisor was Fred Dahl, and the production supervisor was Suzanne
W. B. Rapcavage. It was set in Palatino by Inkwell Publishing Services.*

Printed and bound by R. R. Donnelley & Sons Company.

*To Jay and Katherine
who have shown
perseverance
and determination
beyond their years.*

Contents

Preface

On a plane to Washington, DC, recently, we overheard a conversation between two executives in front of us. One was a woman on her way to a job interview for a position she really wanted in a prestigious law firm. It was clear from her comments that she had done all the right things up to this point. She had an excellent background, had prepared well, and had networked her way into this interview. Yet she was visibly nervous.

The other executive told her that, although it had been over ten years since he had changed positions, he felt sure his interviewing methods were still successful. He stressed being fully prepared for questions about education and professional experience. She said she was and proved it by being able to answer the questions he asked her.

After grilling her for some time he pronounced, "Terrific, you really are prepared. The key to your interview is your ability to react quickly and give the best possible response to the interviewer's question."

The man's remarks were encouraging but off the mark. Thorough knowledge of your education and work history and being quick on your feet all help you win a position, given enough opportunities. But this sounded like a position the woman *really* wanted—the kind of job that comes only once or twice in a career. This was the killer interview, and she would have to do a lot more than follow the advice she had heard.

This incident more than anything else finally convinced us to listen to the words of friends and colleagues and write this book.

As we talk with managers and executives from many different companies, we hear a recurring theme: Making the right choice in key hires is more important than ever before. Global competition has caused a reevaluation of recruiting and hiring practices. Interviewers understand the critical financial implications of good and bad hires and are expanding their hiring teams—the goal being to achieve consensus before making a job offer. The difference between the successful candidate and the rest is often extremely small.

Executives who have reached the top have learned to play the interview game. They successfully employ the strategies to win the killer interviews. We have distilled these successful concepts and incorporated them into a comprehensive yet straightforward strategy that enables you to land the best job in today's extremely competitive business marketplace. This book is intended for executives and aspiring executives who expect crucial interviews to be part of their successful career paths in business, education, not-for-profit, or government.

Success involves creating synergy in a win-win environment, where both interviewer and job seeker can successfully complete their agendas. This may sound easy but it requires the knowledge of a strategic game plan, managed and implemented in the style of an aggressive executive or professional coach. A major benefit of the strategy is that it enables you to evaluate your behavior during the interview and make the subtle adjustments to push you over the top.

When winning the job through a series of interviews, successful executives ask the right questions and evaluate the answers to make the best "buy" decision. The buy section of this book is invaluable in helping you analyze whether this company is the right place for you to enjoy yourself, provide for you and your family, and maximize your career growth.

In summary, key corporate players tell you that the most qualified candidate, based on academic background, skills and accomplishments, doesn't always, or even usually, win the job. How you handle rapport building and presentation in the interview is equally important to, if not more important than, building the interviewer's confidence that you are the best fit in the organization. *This book provides you with the strategic game plan to instill great confidence when you enter a critical interview.* We invite you to read on and learn the skills to move forward successfully in your business career.

FREDERICK W. BALL
BARBARA B. BALL

Acknowledgments

We are grateful to a few close friends and colleagues who gave us counsel and support in the development and production of the book. Louis Wolfe, former CEO of Bantam Books, Inc., served as our mentor throughout the process. He patiently took the time to answer the uncountable questions from two authors navigating in new waters; he spent many hours reading and critiquing the drafts of the book. Bill McCord, a partner in an investment firm and an expert in due diligence, contributed a great deal to the study job applicants undertake when deciding whether the company is right for them. Bill also gave us invaluable counsel and encouragement on other portions of the book.

Dr. Bill Brittain, a psychologist and principal in his own human resource consulting firm, contributed much toward the chapter on the interviewer's agenda. Bob Gilbert, chairman of a San Francisco–based human resource firm, provided valuable insights regarding strategies. Bob Littmann, president and CEO of an air and water purification company, offered an entrepreneur's perspective and sustained us with unflagging belief in our vision. Jaye Smith, a managing director in a New York human resource firm and an adjunct professor at New York University, analyzed the book for its content. Rick Miners, a principal in his own executive search firm, assessed the book for its practical application.

We also owe thanks to Andy Sherwood, the CEO of Goodrich & Sherwood, for his advice and encouragement. Gren Paynter, a senior consultant with the same firm, refined the content and made suggestions regarding style. We also appreciate the support and interest of our colleagues at G&S.

Kathy Trager, a publishing attorney, helped us understand the intricacies of creating a book. Ken Collins, a partner in an executive search firm, guided us on the publishing path, and Steve Rivkin, president of a marketing and communications consulting firm and coauthor of *The New Positioning* (McGraw-Hill, 1995) introduced us to his publisher.

Betsy Brown, our Senior Editor at McGraw-Hill, gave valuable suggestions and support. Bob Hild and Karen Stark, expert computer consultants, designed the figures and made other significant contributions.

Finally, we feel a deep sense of gratitude to our children, Jay and Katherine, who patiently endured the creation of this book.

PART 1

The Tough Business of Interviewing

1

The Competition in the Marketplace

The successful techniques that you are about to learn have helped hundreds of executives and managers win the jobs they really wanted. When asked why our interview strategies were effective, one executive said, "It was just incredible. I felt like I was the director of a play. Not only did I know the script cold, I could also still make subtle adjustments to make the play outstanding." After reading this book, you too will understand the strategies of an interview inside and out, and will have the skills to fine-tune an interview while you're there.

Recently, a friend made a job change. He was the vice-president of finance for a Fortune 1000 company and was looking for a similar position with another company. With an undergraduate degree in engineering and an MBA in finance from a top school, he obviously had a great background. When he landed his new position as CFO of a larger company, we asked him for his strongest reactions to his job search. We were surprised when he said without hesitation:

> I never thought there would be so many excellent candidates out there. I guess I thought I'd be competing in a small pool, but there are many people just like me and the differences between candidates seem minute. The CEO of my new company told me that it was my last three interviews, not my credentials, that set me apart.

Interviewing for a job is serious business. Nobody needs to tell you that it's very competitive out there. And it's becoming more competitive. Since landing a new job is tough—maybe even tougher than performing in the position you'll ultimately take—it's critical to understand everything you can about interviewing. In addition, self-confidence is a critical factor to lift you to success. Basketball superstar Michael Jordan is well-known for his total dedication to the game and his overwhelming confidence in his own ability. He believes he can do anything on the court and no one can stop him. That kind of confidence is the foundation of an impenetrable self-concept that distinguishes the great basketball player from the good one, the great job candidate from the good one.

It's an old maxim that the more prepared you are, the more confident you'll be. In this book we'll walk you through each step necessary to prepare for killer interviews. Part 1 sets the stage with a discussion of competitiveness in the marketplace, the need to have a strategy if you are to be successful, and the strength of your will to win.

Part 2 deals with the preparation needed before you enter the competition. Psychological, physical, and intellectual preparation take time, thought, and determination. It is easy to rationalize:

"I can demonstrate confidence in an interview [regardless of how I feel in general]."

"I am a high-energy person [despite being 15 pounds overweight and unable to remain focused by the third consecutive interview]."

"I am able to discuss any facet of my skills and abilities in detail [despite my inability to cut to the heart of the matter by citing specific competencies and defending them with appropriate accomplishments]."

Those who are prepared propel themselves to a new and higher plateau where there are fewer candidates and better job opportunities.

Once you're prepared, Part 3 helps you to understand the fabric of the interview. It is critical:

1. To build rapport with the interviewer.

2. But it is also important to help the interviewer accomplish her objectives in the interview. It is one thing to understand intellectually the need to help the other person, but it is another thing to actually *do* it. Skills such as listening, problem solving, formulating solutions, and presenting are keys to success.

3. The truly successful job applicant, however, must balance the needs of the interviewer with the need to accomplish his own objectives as well. This third need significantly adds to the complexity of the task, but, if handled effectively, it dramatically increases the chances for success.

After looking at the interview from the interviewer's and the candidate's perspectives, we'll examine how to create win-win interaction and effective interview strategies. Finally, you'll learn how to evaluate your performance.

Part 4 helps you to select the right company. While the company is determining whether you are the best fit for the position, *you* should be doing your own investigation to decide whether this is the best position for you, your family, and your career. Due to its importance, the buy side investigation (this is where you become the buyer) should start as early as possible and run concurrently with the sell side activities (when you are selling your abilities). In addition to selecting the right company, you want to negotiate the best and fairest offer.

If you haven't begun to look for a job yet or if it's early in your job campaign, you should follow the book sequentially. This enables you to prepare properly before getting too far into the campaign. If, however, you are already involved in one or more interviews, then you may want to begin at Part 3 which deals with the dynamics of the interview. Finally, if you have an offer in hand and want to evaluate it, then we suggest you begin at Part 4, selecting the right company.

2
The Need for a Game Plan

Have you ever stopped to think how you got where you are today in your career? Why you picked the job function? Or the industry? Or the geographic location? The majority of people make career decisions in amazing ways. You'll hear comments like:

"I sort of fell into this job."

"I always wanted to live on the West Coast."

"X [a well-known company] recruited on my campus."

"I did what my family expected."

"I saw a movie (or read a book) once and Y seemed like a good job."

Many people don't think much about career decisions. They often just happen.

If people often don't have a plan for charting their careers, they do seem to have a strategy for interviewing. Why, then, is there an issue? *Because the strategies that people develop are often off base, sometimes drastically so.*

A major mistake is to assume that former job hunting experience alone or a successful interview you may have had for a part-time job during college are enough to assist you. Heavy reliance on experience might be fine if you are the same person you were the last time you looked for a job (in terms of age, skills, interests) and if the job market has not changed. This, obviously, won't be the case.

Suppose you landed your first position quickly by interviewing with a friend of the family. The job interview consisted of talking about comfortable topics (family, sailing, skiing, and mutual friends), after which there was a brief discussion of your skills and then a job offer. Or suppose that your last job came through a search firm where the search consultant did most of the preliminary work. All you did was show up for the interview. In addition, suppose that your potential boss had heard wonderful things about you and spent most of the job interview "selling" you on the company. You, in a sense, reversed roles and became the "buyer."

CAREER PROFILE
Effortless Landing

Or suppose you landed as I (Fred) did early in my career. I had been a high school science teacher and basketball coach, and at 26, I was interested in becoming a school principal. Harry, the superintendent of schools, interviewed me; we liked one another immediately, and in a short time I was hired. I was amazed at the speed of the process.

A few months later at a social event I (Barbara) met the superintendent's wife. She was quite interested to meet me and we chatted for awhile. Eventually, she filled me in on the real story of how Fred had been hired. Harry was new to the school district and he needed a principal. The group of applicants had been screened to a manageable number. He brought their resumes home one afternoon, left them on the kitchen counter, and went out to play tennis with his children.

When he came home his wife greeted him with a big smile, and the news that she had found the new principal. Harry was surprised, to say the least. She explained that when she saw the resumes, she got curious. She started to thumb through them, and when she reached Fred's, she read it and placed it on top.

"Harry, he is born and raised in New Jersey like you are, he is as young as you were when you first started in administration, and he likes tennis like you do. And," she teased, "think how an All-State ball player could help your faculty basketball team!" Harry interviewed other candidates, but his wife was convinced that he decided on Fred then and there.   ❏

What do these successful job searches have in common? Clearly, they are all painless; in these three instances, it obviously feels terrific to be romanced by people who want you. In addition, no strategy is needed at all because the job just falls into your lap. The likelihood of being offered a job as if it were a gift is like hitting the lottery. Sure, it happens, but the odds are that it won't. These are the exceptions rather than the rule. Developing a job hunting and interview plan based on this type of experience often leads to a very frustrating result (unless you have another family friend who just happens to need someone).

We have a family tradition of reading to our kids before bedtime. A line from one of our daughter's favorites, *Alice in Wonderland,* stands out, probably because we have read this book an uncountable number of times in the last ten years. Alice is trying her hardest to get out of a maze when the Cheshire Cat appears and advises her, "If you don't know where you're going, then what does it matter what road you take?"

Job Searches without a Game Plan

A few of our early job searches put us in the same maze as Alice. We had no interviewing strategies whatsoever. We came out of some interviews, for instance, having no idea where we started, where we traveled, or where we ended. Amazingly, in some of those interviews we were successful, but others were disasters. We had no clue what was happening except that we were being asked to answer a lot of questions.

We were oblivious to another aspect of the interview process as well, that of understanding the interviewer's agenda. To be honest, most people never even give that a moment's thought. Help interviewers with their agenda? The assumption is that, since they have the job, are in their own surroundings, and can control the interview, they don't need any help.

Certainly we have both been on interviews where the interviewer was introverted and conversation was dying fast, right along with the chances of getting a job. At that moment intuition took over and we were able to do something to keep it going. But that was different. Neither of us walked into an interview with the idea of helping the interviewer; it just happened. This notion of helping an interviewer to accomplish her business objectives was one we hadn't considered.

Finally, we didn't do very well in making the buy decision of whether to accept an offer. When a potential boss "fell in love" with us, we found ourselves running to accept the job. It was only after being in the position for awhile that questions started to arise like:

"Did anyone ever tell you that the job would be like this?"

"Did you ask enough questions to determine if the boss is a decent person?"

"Why is it that you are finding out now that no one ever gets promoted here?"

"Do you think this company will be in business in a year?"

Proactive Behavior

A number of years ago we entered the career counseling business and guess what we learned about interviewing? We weren't alone. A lot of other people handled job interviews the same way. Bright people. People sophisticated in the ways of business.

That discovery made us stop and think. Maybe these issues were broader than we thought. For many people, interview strategy is generally perceived as having good answers to the interviewer's questions, that is, passive rather than active behavior. Passive seems so wrong.

Some people are afraid proactive behavior will appear too aggressive to the interviewer. While it's true that you can't come at the interviewer like a professional linebacker, we think it's critical to be actively involved in the process. How can you have a productive interview if you can't answer such questions as:

- What are my objectives for the interview?
- How will I determine the organization's needs?
- What will I do to assist the interviewer to understand how I can help solve the organization's problems?
- What do I need to know about the position, my potential boss, the company, the industry? How will I gain this information?
- What other outcomes do I expect from this interview?

When talking about these questions to clients and friends who were interviewing, everyone agreed that having answers to these questions was valuable. No one questioned that. However, the method of acquiring the information was viewed as sensitive—too sensitive for most. We were asked, "How can you exercise influence to get what you need without appearing too aggressive to the person who holds the strings to the job you want?"

The concern is a valid one. If exercising influence is viewed as a power play to take over the interview, then the candidate is in deep trouble. On the other hand, the result can be extremely positive if exercising influence is viewed as an honest attempt to understand and discuss the organization's business problems and how the candidate could be helpful.

We believe that the latter is possible and that a clear, simple strategy for interviewing includes three basic objectives:

Objective 1: Recognize the importance of building rapport.

Objective 2: Accomplish the interviewer's agenda.

Objective 3: Accomplish the candidate's agenda.

Being proactive in the interview fits perfectly into the third objective. If you can learn enough about the company, its direction, goals, and management, you are in a position to conduct a business discussion. In this subtle switch from question and answer to business discussion, you become an equal partner in the conversation. As the discussion centers on the company's business problems, opportunities arise to sell your skills to resolve those problems.

Finally, career counseling has taught us that the job market is tough, the competition is fierce, and the differences between highly qualified candidates are often minuscule. What often pulls the winner over the top is preparation.

Summary

A clear, simple strategy for interviewing includes three basic objectives:

- *Objective 1:* Recognize the importance of building rapport.
- *Objective 2:* Accomplish the interviewer's agenda.
- *Objective 3:* Accomplish the candidate's agenda.

What cannot be overlooked or underestimated is psychological, physical, and intellectual preparation. Those who understand the fierceness of the competition and who are totally prepared will be successful.

PART 2

Smart Preparation

Clear Your Head

Elizabeth, a bright, energetic young accountant, met Bruce, the first of a series of interviewers for a new position. The interview went extremely well until Bruce asked Elizabeth why she was interested in leaving her present company. Elizabeth's head told her to keep her remarks general and not say anything negative about her boss. She spoke of the general environment in her department, which wasn't action-oriented or progressive. Bruce remained silent; after a few seconds, the silence grew uncomfortable for Elizabeth and her nervousness made her feel like she had to fill the void. She blurted, "My boss is very difficult. He is a nice person but he has a 'don't make waves' attitude. No one can take initiative without his approval and he rarely gives it. The situation is intolerable." Elizabeth was embarrassed when she realized that she had violated a basic interviewing rule of never bashing one's boss or company. She knew better but she had been surprised and psychologically unprepared.

The next day the interviewers got together to summarize their thoughts about Elizabeth. The feedback was excellent. She was one of a few preferred candidates. When it was Bruce's turn to give his impressions, he said, "You know, I really liked Elizabeth. There was only one thing she said that concerned me...." Final decisions often come down to reactions like this. She didn't get the job.

Is it possible to prepare for every eventuality in an interview? Probably not, but it is possible to be ready for all major issues and categories of questions. The more thought and preparation that occur prior to an interview, the less is the likelihood that a poor response or series of responses will eliminate you. Does this process really come down to verbal exchanges? Absolutely. Do individuals win or lose jobs because of preparation? Yes. The goal is to be so well prepared for an interview that no question by the interviewer can evoke an unprepared or ill-prepared response. This requires psychological, physical, and intellectual preparation.

The case for preparation is overwhelming. Prepare, prepare, prepare is to interviewing what location, location, location is to real estate. It is critical to success. Unfortunately, preparation is often seen not in the larger context of being an integral part of interview planning, but as a specific, last-minute act to cram in a few facts. You'll sometimes hear, "I don't need much preparation. I'm extremely agile in an interview." This is a formula for a candidate to be turned down for an excellent opportunity, only later to discover he was perceived as arrogant, shallow, or ill prepared. Psychological, physical, and intellectual preparation needs to be launched on the same day as the decision to seek employment or to change positions.

When preparation is undertaken early in the campaign, every aspect of the interviewing process can be addressed. Spending time thinking about an interview gives you an opportunity to develop and fine-tune your approach to various issues. An interview consists of exchanging thousands of words with each person you meet. So the choice between two very competitive candidates often swings on abbreviated exchanges of a few words each.

Fears Associated with Changing Jobs

There is clearly a win/lose aspect to a job campaign that causes emotional highs and lows. Self-confidence can be high at one moment and low at another. That happens to every person who has ever entered the job market, regardless of level or function or personal circumstances. During low points, fears and questions associated with a job change creep into your mind. Fears fit into a number of general categories, and, once they are understood, it is possible to understand how your inner strength will overcome them.

1. Lack of Self-confidence

Your view of self is so closely tied to job success that, if you are looking for your first job, are between jobs, or are unhappy in your present job, your self-concept is affected. Whatever the reason, the effect can be the same.

Questions
- Am I prepared for the rigors of interviewing?
- Will I maintain my sense of purpose?

- Will I maintain my self-respect?
- Will I be able to support my family?
- Will the new people I meet while networking or interviewing be friendly?

2. Negative Reactions

The fear is that family, friends, and business associates will react negatively to your situation. In the same way that self-concept is often measured by job success, the reaction of others is another way that people measure how they are doing. On the business side, your associates may have seen you only as successful and moving up the career ladder. How will they react now? On the personal side, one wonders how family and friends will react to the prospect of a job change.

Questions
- Will my family support me through this process?
- Will they understand that getting a job offer takes time?
- Do they understand that I need the right job, not just a job?
- Will my friends desert me at a time when I need them?
- Will my business associates understand why I am looking for a new position?
- How will associates react if I do not attain the level of position I am seeking?

3. Derailment of Career Path

As companies have become leaner and more competitive, layers of middle management and staff functions have been eliminated. This may mean fewer clear-cut promotional positions and an even more acute trend in this direction in the future. In the past, when someone entered a career path, a fairly clear trail was defined. In some consumer products companies, for example, the path was so clear that you would know the number of months to the next promotion, assuming good performance evaluations. Looking ahead, however, steady advancement may not be the case. Lateral moves may have to supplant hierarchal moves at some points on the career ladder. This raises many concerns for job changers.

Questions
- Will my work be challenging and satisfying?
- Will finding the right job be extremely difficult?

- Will my career progress be slowed by a job change?
- How can I predict whether my next company will survive?
- How will I evaluate my potential fit with my next boss?
- Will I have an opportunity to move within my new company?
- Can I achieve a promotion by moving to a new company?

4. The Unknown

This fear surfaces when an individual enters the job market for the first time or reenters after an absence. If you are entering for the first time, you normally feel apprehensive about facing a new or different challenge. If you are entering the job market after being away from it, your concerns are with market conditions at this time and your marketability.

Questions

- Is the job market more difficult now than when I last searched for a job?
- Will I be able to secure a position within a given time frame?
- How do I approach a job interview in this climate?
- Am I too young/old, inexperienced/overqualified, generalized/specialized?
- Am I marketable?

Positive Characteristics

If these fears could not be overcome, this would be a depressing chapter. Fortunately, that's not the case. Preparation, along with knowledge of interviewing skills and strategies, builds self-confidence. And that self-confidence snowballs. When you have your first good interview, you build additional confidence. You begin to realize that the skills and abilities you have developed, which often go unnoticed in daily routines, have moved you to a higher ability level. When an interviewer expresses interest in you (whether you receive an offer or not), it makes you stronger for the next round of interviews. A set of inner strengths and characteristics begins to take over.

1. Overwhelmingly Positive Attitude

It is generally held that people who have positive attitudes can truthfully say such things as:

- "I am glad to be alive."
- "I am capable of anything I set my mind to."
- "I use my thoughts, emotions, actions, and time wisely."
- "I give myself time to reflect."

All of us would love to be highly positive 100 percent of the time. But, since we are human, we have some ups and downs. On down days it may be helpful to have a positive model.

Your model could be anybody. I (Fred) still think of Jimmy Connors before I serve a big point in a tennis match. Jimmy would look you in the eye, tell you where he was going to hit the ball, hit the ball there, and beat you anyway because he didn't believe he could lose the point.

It is a given that most people would rather work with a "positive, can-do, let's make it happen" person. Job candidates know the importance of being positive. Despite their best intentions, however, many candidates, if given enough time, tend to volunteer negatives or perceived negatives about themselves. This happens at all levels, from recent graduates to corporation presidents, in as many ways as you can imagine. When asked why he took a specific job, a candidate might respond, "I took my previous job with XYZ company because I felt it would give me excellent experience, better even than if I had attained an MBA." Did anyone ask about graduate work? No. But the person's perception was that there was a weakness due to the lack of a graduate degree. The issue might never have entered the interviewer's mind, but now it is a potential negative thrown on the table by the job applicant.

Why does this happen? It is probably because many of us have been brought up with the notion that humility is a virtue, and, in an effort to give "full disclosure," we volunteer negatives. We have no quarrel with honesty—it is absolutely essential. But *an interview is not the place to be self-effacing*, especially if you are not even asked to comment on the topic.

You simply cannot allow negative thoughts or actions to infiltrate your presentation. You must be consistently positive in selling your strongest skills and abilities.

2. Total Commitment to the Task

Commitment requires that:

- You understand your goals.
- You believe the task is consistent with your values.
- You accept what needs to be accomplished.
- You have the spirit and the will to succeed.

What degree of commitment is necessary to land a new position? You need a good deal more than most people think. Once you have defined a position, commitment and enthusiasm are critical to your success in the interview. Any good interviewer is looking for signs that indicate an interest and enthusiasm for the work.

Commitment is almost always visible to a knowledgeable interviewer. So is a lack of commitment. Not always consciously, but somehow in the course of an interview, the signals will be broadcast. While the following incident eventually has a happy ending, it clearly illustrates how visible the candidate's interest is to the interviewer.

CAREER PROFILE
Conflicting Emotions

A divorce made it impossible for Bob to remain as a senior officer in his former father-in-law's building products firm. He thought about working for another building products company, but he also had interest in other industries, such as sporting equipment or apparel. Since his background was sales and marketing, Bob did not feel restricted. He was also interested in living in three or four different areas of the country.

Soon an interesting possibility surfaced. Daniel, a longtime friend and owner of his own building products company for over 50 years, decided it was time for him to pass the mantle of running his company to a younger person. As he spoke with friends regarding a potential successor, someone mentioned Bob. Daniel was very excited about the possibility. Bob met with Daniel on a number of occasions and the meetings went extremely well.

At a dinner meeting, Daniel asked Bob about career goals and desires. Since he had known Daniel a long time, Bob was open and candid. He mentioned the geographic areas where he might like to live, the types of companies he was exploring, and the fact that he would like to be the president of a company. Most of the wish list included more exotic types of work in more exotic places. He, however, remained very interested in the company and let Daniel know. Dinner concluded on a warm, congenial note.

A few weeks later Daniel called Bob and told him that he had selected another candidate to be the president of his company. Bob was dumbfounded. He caught his breath and asked Daniel what he had done wrong. "Absolutely nothing," Daniel told him. During the conversation Daniel told Bob that he was the ideal candidate. Daniel needed a president with a sales and marketing background and Bob fit the bill perfectly. And the fact that Bob came from the building products field was like icing on the cake. They had known each other for years, and Daniel knew the chemistry would be good. Why, then, was Bob not chosen?

Daniel explained that he started the company with his own sweat and built it into a success over the years. He was committed to the company and he loved it. He needed someone else who showed that he could feel the same way, and Bob didn't. Bob had other things that he needed to do, and it was clear to Daniel that they did not include this company, at this time, and in this place. So Daniel picked someone who was less qualified but more committed.

What was visible to Daniel was a surprise to Bob; he hadn't realized that his ambivalence about what he wanted to do with his life was so apparent. For a few weeks Bob was devastated. He questioned whether he should have tried to fake the commitment to get the job. Within a short time, however, he landed an exciting position in the sports equipment industry in one of the areas of the country he had targeted. He hadn't realized how badly he needed a change, and had not expected how excited (and committed) he became in a new industry and with a new company.   ❏

3. An Intelligent, Organized Game Plan

A game plan can be divided into logical objectives:

- You will identify what needs to be done.
- You will schedule time wisely.
- You will manage time to meet deadlines.
- You will evaluate results and make changes as necessary.

Organization is a critical ingredient to success. As you begin your physical preparation, you need a specific workout regimen that includes three to six workouts per week. Intellectual preparation requires organization to identify your major skill sets and to determine the accomplishments that best illustrate your skills.

Then you need to be organized as you identify the target companies you plan to pursue. Once you are asked to appear for an interview, you need to research the position, the company, the products and/or services, and the people. This may require seeking information from the company, identifying and speaking with people who know about the company, library research, or any other means of obtaining information. At the conclusion of your first round of interviews, it takes discipline and organization to send thank you letters promptly.

When you're called for a second round of interviews, you'll need to learn as much as possible about the people interviewing you (both personally and professionally). In addition, if you can gather more information about the company, study it and develop a list of questions to help you in your study of the company.

After the interview, continue your due diligence activities, checking with individuals who know about the company such as suppliers or customers, employees, consultants, bankers, lawyers, and accountants. The more thorough your due diligence is, the less the chance for surprises and the greater the chance for success.

4. Perseverance and Determination

The actions associated with perseverance and determination are:

- You will act now.
- You will stretch yourself.
- You will learn from your experience and mistakes.
- You won't quit until you succeed.

Of these characteristics, we are convinced that "You will act now" and "You won't quit until you succeed" matter most. In a job campaign, just as with any other challenge in life, there will be peaks and valleys. Fred's dad kept a quotation attributed to Calvin Coolidge on his desk for years that got him through some rough times:

> Nothing can take the place of persistence in the world. Talent will not; nothing is more common than unsuccessful men with talent. Genius will not; unrewarded genius is almost a proverb. Education alone will not; the world is full of educated failures. Persistence and determination alone are omnipotent.

It's stories of people dealing with adversity that make abstract concepts like perseverance and determination hit home. We believe in the power of role models or heroes as inspiration to help us rise to a challenge and be successful. When students in various urban schools were asked for their heroes, they named sports giants like David Robinson of the San Antonio Spurs and Larry Bird, formerly of the Boston Celtics, and celebrities like Oprah Winfrey. When asked why heroes matter, their answers were simple: They work hours and weeks and years until they are the best. They overcome adversity. They never give up. What these students seem to be saying is that heroes are proof that any task can be accomplished if there is a strong enough belief and desire to accomplish the goal.

CAREER PROFILE
Real Hero

How could Jeff Blatnick be anything except a real live hero? Blatnick hoped to be a Greco-Roman wrestler for the United States Olympic team. Two years before the 1984 Olympics, he was weight lifting when he discovered several lumps in his neck. He went to his family physician in Schenectady, New York, who gave him the diagnosis of Hodgkins disease. Within a month, doctors had removed his spleen and started him on radiation therapy. No one believed he would compete again, let alone in the Olympics.

Blatnick went through all the emotional reactions you can imagine, but he overcame all of the negative emotions. He made the decision that he was going to beat this new opponent as decisively as he had defeated all the wrestlers throughout his career. He began to work out again, enduring the rigors of Olympic training while fighting to overcome cancer. Was he superhuman? No. Blatnick was not superhuman, but he was determined to reach his goal by training relentlessly. He moved out of the house so his parents wouldn't see the pain he endured.

Perseverance paid off. Blatnick made the Olympic team and won the starting position in the super heavyweight division. The rest is straight out of a storybook except that it is true. Along the way he upset a Yugoslav, defeated a Greek who was so desperate that he bit him in the hand during the match, and won the Gold Medal with a victory over a Swede. There can't be many better examples of the power of perseverance and determination than Jeff Blatnick's journey. But there are uncountable numbers of everyday people who triumph because of perseverance and determination. Look for your own heroes. They're out there. ❑

5. Impenetrable Self-confidence

The aspects of impenetrable self-confidence are:

- You will succeed because you have prepared extremely well.
- You will succeed because you have an outstanding game plan.
- You will succeed because you believe you will succeed.

Impenetrable self-confidence is the degree to which you believe in yourself. Entering the job market can be scary. On the one hand, your life successes give you strength and confidence. On the other hand, there may be a self-appointed critic behind every bush who is willing to look at your career and make suggestions. Too often, they are negative or incorrect.

You combat this with impenetrable self-confidence. Once you have done your homework and selected a realistic, attainable target, move ahead. Don't let anyone discourage you from reaching the goal. Push on. It may take some time, but success will follow.

CAREER PROFILE
Proactive Game Plan

Gordon was a vice-president for administration with a small company that was headed nowhere. The level of challenge in his position diminished as the organization cut back. Gordon reasoned that he could try to hang on as long as possible or strike out in positive new directions. Never one to sit on his hands, he worked out a severance arrangement with his company and set out in new directions.

After some career self-assessment, he determined that law firm administration was a position whose time had come and that such a position represented an ideal use of his skills. The fact that it would be considered a career change by many people did not deter him in any way.

As Gordon talked to others about his interest, he became more excited about the new field. At the same time, all the negatives were thrown at him. Friends and colleagues who meant well reminded him that he had little experience in the service industry; he was 50 years old and living in a very competitive metropolitan area. Gordon listened and absorbed what he needed to know, learning what negatives he would face when he approached the marketplace.

Then he rejected all the negative thoughts. With great excitement, motivation, commitment, and self-confidence he moved ahead. He worked tirelessly and more enthusiastically than any of his friends imagined possible.

He was rejected from consideration by some firms prior to an interview because his resume showed no law firm experience. He was rejected in others after one interview. And he was rejected by a few firms in the final selection because they could not quite

---

KEYS TO INTERVIEWING SUCCESS

If you have an overwhelmingly positive attitude and are committed to a realistic and worthwhile goal, and if you pursue it with organization, perseverance, determination, and impenetrable self-confidence, then you will be successful.

---

convince themselves to take a chance on someone with good ideas but no experience. In each case, however, Gordon received reinforcement that his personal and professional characteristics were appropriate for a law firm. Success required just one firm willing to take a risk.

While other job applicants passively waited for a call back, Gordon was in touch with each potential employer as often as possible without alienating anyone. He wasn't bashful about telling his contact how excited he was about law firm administration and the possibility of their working together. He asked if additional information was required or if the firm had undertaken a current project that might require his expertise.

When Gordon landed his position as a law firm administrator in a Chicago law firm, his new employer told him that his commitment and enthusiasm in his approach to life and to their firm were the deciding factors in their decision to hire him. The other major consideration was his self-confidence, which convinced the partners that he would be successful in accomplishing his new duties.   ❑

Summary

The internal strengths that you can call on are:

- Overwhelmingly positive attitude.
- Total commitment to the task.
- Intelligent, organized game plan.
- Perseverance and determination.
- Impenetrable self-confidence.

Taken together, these extremely powerful strengths can be used to overcome any fears or concerns that surface. The bottom line is simple. If you have an overwhelmingly positive attitude and are committed to a realistic and worthwhile goal, and if you pursue it with organization, perseverance, determination, and impenetrable self-confidence, then you will be successful.

STEP 2

Become
Physically Fit

Physical exercise is not often mentioned in connection with preparation for a job campaign and interviewing. It should be. Since physical preparation is a critical element in landing a job, it's important to start conditioning as early as possible.

It is critical to look physically fit in the job interview. The first thing that an interviewer observes—before a word is spoken, before anything else happens—is physical appearance. And the first value judgment is fit and trim, or too heavy? And, *like it or not*, clear value judgments go with each category. Trimness and fitness create a perception of self-confidence, discipline, energy, and drive. Heaviness carries the opposite tag of low self-confidence, lack of energy, and no drive. We don't agree with these reactions or condone them, but many feel that an overweight condition is evidence of a lack of professionalism.

Do these thoughts actually occur to interviewers? Absolutely. Do they affect the decision making process? Yes. Are they fair? Immaterial. Physical appearance is part of an important first impression.

Informal Survey

So let's take stock. Do most people need to lose at least a few pounds? Take an informal survey. At a restaurant, during a sporting event, in your company, or on the street, analyze the first 20 adults who walk by. Now ask yourself, what percentage are 10 pounds or more overweight? Sixty percent? Seventy-five percent? Eighty percent? Americans talk a good game about fitness (and athletic equipment and clothing companies are major success stories because Americans love to look the part of an athlete). The fact, however, is that millions of Americans are far from fit. Incidentally, your conclusions from this informal survey will mirror the statistics of the population as a whole. If you are overweight, attack the problem early under the advice and direction of your family physician.

If you do your own survey, it becomes clear that, when you enter an interview physically fit, you are in a better position than a large percentage of the candidate population. At worst, you are competitive. At best, you are ahead of many or most of the other candidates.

The longer-term effects can also be extremely positive. Ask anyone who is physically fit or who has recently attained that state through weight loss and a physical exercise program how they feel. You hear, "wonderful," "great," "terrific." Now add outstanding business attire. The result is usually an individual who has an extremely positive attitude and a high degree of self-confidence. And why not? A turnaround can be dramatic.

CAREER PROFILE
Getting Your Life in Order

Evan was an extremely effective product manager. He had all the necessary technical and interpersonal skills. He was clearly a rising star in the organization. His painful separation from one of the organization's senior managers changed all that. The personal aspects of the situation took a greater toll on him emotionally than Evan thought possible. He was depressed, tough to live with, gaining weight, and generally deteriorating.

Things didn't go much better professionally. People at work tended to take sides, and, since his estranged wife was a senior manager, more people sided with her. Evan saw the handwriting on the wall and he decided to attack the problem head on. He went to see his boss and told him that things didn't seem to be working out. Evan asked him if he could help him secure a severance package. His boss was helpful and Evan left.

It took Evan a few months to allow the healing process to take place. When he was feeling better, he started to become excited about finding a new position. However, a friend gave him the sobering news that he had become overweight and looked sloppy. Evan hadn't given his appearance much thought, but, when he looked in the mirror, he had to agree. He immediately attacked the weight problem the way he had attacked work—with a vengeance. It took some time but he started to lose the weight.

Evan was astonished by the direct correlation between the cumulative weight loss and the return of his self-confidence. When his weight reached the appropriate level, he bought a new suit for interviewing; he knew he looked his best and he felt great. He landed a new, exciting position shortly thereafter.   ❏

Initial impression is reason enough to approach an interview fit and trim. The first impression is an important one. But what happens over the course of the entire interview or interviews is also extremely important. Is interviewing physically exhausting? Ask anyone who has interviewed recently. The answer is a resounding "yes!" Now suppose that, instead of one interview, there are two, three, four, or more interviews on the same day.

The need for physical fitness during multiple interviews is interesting. No doubt, some firms feel energy and drive are critical elements in the success quotient for a position. One means for them to test these characteristics is to schedule multiple interviews deliberately on the same day. More often than not, however, in this era of "lean and mean" operations, scheduling multiple interviews is a necessity when the interviewing executives are in town or can cut themselves loose from other meetings. Multiple interviews are exhausting and require excellent physical conditioning, as well as mental preparation.

Mental Alertness

Along with outstanding physical conditioning, mental alertness is another function of an exercise program. Physical conditioning and mental alertness go hand in hand. You must be as physically prepared and as mentally alert at the end of your last interview (perhaps five o'clock on a Friday afternoon) as you were at the beginning of your first interview. Mental alertness furnishes the energy and stamina required to remain positive and focused through one or more interviews.

A major component is the ability to listen. University studies show that most adults stay plugged in attentively to a conversation for less than two minutes before their attention is diverted. Be honest. Don't you find that when a family member or friend starts to speak, you either tune in or tune out depending on your interest in the subject? Remember being in a class at college and realizing that your mind was wandering? You had no idea what the professor had been lecturing about for several minutes (or even longer if the subject matter wasn't very high on your list of all-time favorites).

In interviewing, unfortunately, you can't do that. Instead of listening selectively, you must remain focused as close to 100 percent of the time as possible. Active listening results in a response that is clear, crisp, and right to the point. A major concern of the interviewer is whether the applicant listens and responds directly to the question.

Another equally important reason for remaining focused is that you have your own agenda in the interview as well. Accomplishing your agenda requires careful listening, needs development, and the application of creative problem solving skills.

Aerobic Exercise

To achieve physical conditioning, then, the best systems are the aerobic exercise programs, and the best exercises are swimming, bicycling, walking, and/or jogging. This is not a haphazard once-in-awhile program, but a systematic three to six times a week regimen. As with any plan, it is important to build up slowly until you reach full strength. Exercise more times per week rather than less. The schedule should start on the first day that you decide to seek a job or job change, and it should continue throughout your campaign. (*Note:* Any exercise program should be conducted under the direction of your doctor.)

Your routine helps you to be in outstanding physical shape when you are called for interviews. Working out on the day of the interview can also assist you to relax and remain focused. How much should you exercise on that day? Certainly you should do no more than you have been doing in your regular program. You want to do enough to relax but not so much that you tire yourself. With the appropriate amount of exercise, your head is clearer, and you keep the interview in perspective.

The notion of physical activity before something important is not new. In acting, for example, it is commonplace. A new female lead had been hired for a highly successful Broadway play, and it was her first night. She was so nervous that she was almost ill, and she was afraid that she wouldn't be able to perform. Instinctively, she began to walk. She found herself in the deep shadows behind the stage. As her eyes adjusted to the dark she thought she saw a person in the corner. It was the star of the show. His legs were spread apart, hands pressed up against the wall, and he was doing exercises. He stopped when he saw her, and realizing how upset she was, he insisted that she join him. Since no one ever said "no" to Yul Brynner, she nervously joined him. Soon the physical exercises relaxed her to the point that she could begin her normal breathing exercises. Her performance was outstanding.

Building in time to exercise on an interview day offers other potential benefits. The additional time it takes allows you to forget the pressures of your present job or activities and to focus on various aspects of the upcoming interview. This time often pays dividends.

CAREER PROFILE
Arriving Early

Charles had an interview for a senior-level college administrative position. His first interview was a dinner meeting at six o'clock with the vice-president and other college officials, followed immediately by a second interview. It took Charles approximately three hours to drive to the campus. Rather than go to work for half a day, Charles decided to arrive early, identify where the meetings would take place, and introduce himself to the secretary who was handling the administrative duties related to the search, and exercise.

When he met the secretary, Charles discovered that they had grown up in the same town and knew a lot of the same people. He suddenly felt as if he had an ally. While they were talking, the vice-president walked by the desk. After introductions, the vice-president said, "I've had an appointment canceled, so why don't you come in for a few minutes." They met for two hours and found that they were very comfortable with one another.

After the meeting, Charles went back to the hotel and then went jogging. He found the dinner much more enjoyable because he knew the vice-president. He was even able to eat. The interviews consisted of speaking with 54 different people, individually or in groups, between Monday evening and Wednesday afternoon. Charles exercised each morning prior to the day's interviews. He gave himself high marks for the three-day performance. Two of the reasons, as he saw them, were the exercise regimen and the fortuitous meeting with the secretary and vice-president. There was another round of interviews later, but Charles was convinced that he won the position in round one. ❏

Summary

An aerobic exercise program (walking, swimming, bicycling, and/or jogging) should be undertaken at the beginning of a job search (under the direction of your doctor) and implemented three to six times per week. The benefits include:

- Good physical appearance.
- Sufficient conditioning to withstand the rigors of interviewing.
- Increases in energy and stamina.
- Relaxation and stress reduction.

Assess Your Competencies and Accomplishments

Intellectual preparation is understanding interview strategies and preparing for the content point of the interview. This type of preparation entails complete knowledge of your skills and abilities, and it is the focus of this chapter. Interview strategies and tactics are the focus later in the book. The thoroughness of your preparation determines the quality of the conversation you'll have with the interviewer. Presentation is also extremely important, but, without content preparation, presentation cannot carry the day.

Preparation is an enigma. On the one hand, job seekers acknowledge the importance of preparation. On the other hand, many of them spend a minimal amount of time analyzing their skills and accomplishments, saying that it's unnecessary because they know themselves and don't need to spend much time in preparation. This is the old "pay me now or pay me later" dilemma. Time spent in preparation clearly pays dividends in the job interview and cuts the time in landing a new position. And, just as critically, preparation dramatically increases the probability that it will be the right job.

If lucky, the unprepared job seeker meets a knowledgeable, professional interviewer early on who shatters the idea that knowing yourself intuitively is synonymous with preparation. We say "lucky" because it is better to learn the lesson very quickly and not lose a great deal of time. The tough questions come with a specific focus that demand direct answers.

For example, "What are your two or three critical abilities that will distinguish you from the other candidates I will meet?" What's really being asked couldn't be clearer! "Why should I hire you? What makes you different?" Some people say that a question like that isn't so tough. They rattle on about "new business generation ... my ability to manage people ... my marketing and research background ... producing quality products at a profit." Wrong answer.

Two to Four Key Competencies (aka Skills)

What's wrong with that answer? It just isn't that easy. For one thing, you better be sure that the two to four competencies you highlight are your best abilities. There is no second chance. Next, be prepared for the interviewer to continue the line of questioning. "That's interesting. Can you give me some specific examples that illustrate each point?" Your examples need to be very specific and include not only what you did but why you saw the need and how you went about accomplishing the task. The bottom line is critical: You need to show how you added value to the company's profitability. You will be asked follow-up questions concerning the bottom line; so be prepared. Plan to explain at least five specific accomplishments to illustrate each competency. Give appropriate details to demonstrate clearly your abilities and still present them succinctly. To help you do this, we have provided a "Competencies and Accomplishments Worksheet" on pages 35–36. The best rule to follow in succinct presentation is the 60-second rule, which comes from sales research: You have 60 seconds to make your point to the interviewer or you will lose your listener.

The interviewer may want to spend time on each one, just have them highlighted, or not deal with them at all. But you must be ready.

You probably have a great number of competencies, but that isn't what you were asked. You were asked to select your *best* competencies—the ones that separate you from other candidates and give you an edge. We recently put this question to a job seeker who sold cash management products for banks. His response was:

THE 60-SECOND RULE

You have 60 seconds to make your point to the interviewer or you will lose your listener.

COMPETENCIES AND ACCOMPLISHMENTS WORKSHEET

The more able you are to help the interviewer understand your competencies and accomplishments, the more convincing your argument is that you have the skills to do the job.

Competencies

What are your three strongest competencies? For example, is it leading people, development and supervision, sending profit to the bottom line, new product development, sales? List the competencies in the space below:

Accomplishments

Define your five strongest accomplishments that support each of the competencies. Write the accomplishments as follows:

Action verb (past tense) → What were you proud of → How it was good for the company (quantify your results in terms of dollars, percentages, or times).

A few examples follow:

- "Created and implemented new computer program that saved $30,000 per year in consulting fees."
- "Generated $200,000 in new business in 18 months."
- "Negotiated 10 labor contracts (payrolls in excess of $50 million) with no work stoppages."

In the following worksheet, list five accomplishments that support the appropriate competency:

Competency 1: _____

_____

_____

Accomplishments:

1. _____

_____

2. _____

_____

3. _____

_____

4. _____

_____

5. _____

_____

Competency 2: _____

_____

_____

Accomplishments:

1. _____

_____

2. _____

_____

3. _____

_____

4. _____

_____

5. _____

_____

Competency 3: _____

_____

Accomplishments:

1. _____

_____

2. _____

_____

3. _____

_____

4. _____

_____

5. _____

_____

Most cash management professionals are technical salespeople who support loan officers. I'm different in that I actually go out and bring in new customers to the bank. Last year I brought in a number of new accounts that resulted in $300,000 in new revenue.

This type of response can differentiate you from other candidates and lead to a position. The more help you can give your potential boss in understanding how your skills can help the company move toward its goals, the greater is the chance you will be hired.

CAREER PROFILE
Effective Packaging

Beth was an economist for a major bank. However, at one point in her life she had worked for a political party. She also had a two-year stint as an account officer in a marketing role. Her firm had a number of Japanese clients, and Beth had developed expertise in Japanese culture and values.

When Beth was asked to explain distinguishing characteristics about herself she said, "I am an economist who has (a) learned about profitability while working as an account officer in new business development, (b) worked for a political party, and (c) developed an interest and knowledge of Japanese affairs." That kind of answer gives an interviewer a more complete picture of Beth than the skeletal response of being an account officer or economist. Beth eventually became a vice-president in a Japanese bank—an excellent fit.❑

Ideal Job

Once you have identified your key competencies, the next step is to define an ideal job at this stage of your career. Our advice is to look at your life and career goals within a given time period, such as the next five years. The complexity of your task varies depending on your life phase and responsibilities. For example, if you are single and just out of school, you may have few constraints and are able to live and work wherever you want. At another phase of life you may have a family with a high school sophomore son and senior daughter. Your career may be well established in a job function that you love. In this case the decision may well be that you need a job in the same or closely allied industry, in the same job function, in the same geographic location. At yet another phase of life you may be looking at your last job before retirement, and you may decide that you'd like to move to the place where you plan to retire and find work there.

Defining an ideal job creates a sounding board against which you will be able to compare real jobs as they surface. You may want to ask yourself the following questions about your life and career goals before formulating a statement of your ideal job.

Life Questions

- How much time do you want to spend with family, spouse, friends, work, leisure time, and religious and community involvement?
- How many hours a day are you willing to work under normal circumstances? Under emergency circumstances?
- Does your spouse work?
- What are his or her career goals and timetable?
- Do you have children? What life phases are they in?
- Is moving to a new location a possibility? Is moving desirable? If yes, to what geographic area?

Career Questions

- Do you see yourself happy in a steady track or do you want a fast track to the top (i.e., greater risk, greater reward)?
- Do you want to work in an industry known for its fast pace and long hours (including weekend work)?
- Do you see yourself working for the department or area that drives the business?
- Could you be happy in another department, perhaps one that doesn't drive the business?
- Do you need to work for one of the top firms in the industry or are other companies an option?
- Can you afford trying a high-risk/high-reward opportunity at this phase of your life or do you need a more stable environment?
- Do you want to work for yourself? Can you work alone?
- Do you have the financial stability and temperament to work for yourself?

Once you have thought about some of the life and career questions that will have an impact on you, write your best thoughts regarding an ideal job on paper. To assist you, we have provided an "Ideal Job Worksheet" with some additional criteria on page 39. Include in your description what each of these criteria means to you (add other criteria that are important to you).

IDEAL JOB WORKSHEET

One way to define your ideal job is to write down what you're looking for in each of the following areas:

- Job satisfaction _____
  _____
  _____

- Personal growth _____
  _____
  _____

- Challenge (of the work) _____
  _____
  _____

- Compensation package _____
  _____
  _____

- Recognition _____
  _____
  _____

- Corporate culture _____
  _____
  _____

- Working environment _____
  _____
  _____

- Geographic preference _____
  _____
  _____

- Career options (within an organization) _____
  _____
  _____

- Life/family constraints _____
  _____
  _____

- People (attitudes of superiors, colleagues, subordinates) ____
  _____
  _____

- Other factors (additional factors of concern to you) _____
  _____
  _____

Let's assume hypothetically that you define your ideal job in the same industry, in the same functional area, and in the same geographic area as a previous job. When you identify such a job and go for an interview, your skills and abilities may be a very close match to the job requirements. Therefore, success can be attained by giving specific examples of your prior accomplishments.

Suppose, on the other hand, you are interested in a position in the same functional area but where your key abilities are not a perfect match with the position specifications. You have experience in perhaps 70 to 80 percent of what the job requires. In this case you need to delve a little deeper into your pool of accomplishments. You need to know the details of each accomplishment backward and forward. The best way to do this is to write them down because you'll think about them and organize them as you write. Your focus for the 70 to 80 percent where you have expertise is still in demonstrating that your prior experience and accomplishments enable you to do this job successfully.

Then there is the matter of the 20 to 30 percent you don't have. You have to persuade the interviewer that you have the potential to do that portion of the job. In all probability you have accomplishments in prior jobs that are close enough to the specifications to convince the interviewer that you can be successful. It is critical to know your accomplishments so well that you can provide the right illustration at the right time.

But suppose the interviewer isn't convinced. Then you have to change gears, from experience to potential. Now you have to dig one level deeper into the reservoir of skills that you've developed over your lifetime. Skills can be used effectively to illustrate your abilities at a broader level than a specific accomplishment. Consequently, "coordinating" could be done in conjunction with a political party, a baseball league schedule, a conference, or a project. "Negotiating" could focus on a dispute among siblings, a place to hold a wedding reception, labor relations, or purchasing a major casino/hotel. *The more you can demonstrate how your skills can help you to do the 20 to 30 percent of the job you haven't done before, the more persuasive you are in an interview.*

CAREER PROFILE
Management Readiness

Malcolm had an MBA with a concentration in marketing and finance. His basic responsibility throughout his career was manufacturing in a food company that produced biscuits and wafers, among other products. He had progressed steadily upward to vice-president of manufacturing. Along the way he spent a short time in finance and two years in marketing positions. Now a man-

> ### THE EXTRA 20–30 PERCENT
> The more you can demonstrate how your skills can help you to do the 20 to 30 percent of the job you haven't done before, the more persuasive you are in an interview.

agement change occurred and the general manager position became available. Malcolm had most of the pieces, but he had never held the full profit and loss responsibilities.

Malcolm prepared long and hard for his interview. He knew that his competition would come from outside the organization because he was the obvious choice if management selected from inside. His problem was that outside candidates would probably have significant profit and loss experience.

During his interview, Malcolm spoke of his knowledge of the industry and of the company, including its history, goals, and aspirations. He discussed his knowledge of the people and how to motivate them to accomplish business objectives. He also concentrated on the breadth of his experience in a number of functional areas.

When the conversation turned to profit and loss, Malcolm discussed his experience in finance and all of the finance-related activities he had managed for the company. In short, he argued that he had demonstrated the skills and gained the experience necessary to do the job even though he had not held the title. Malcolm had done his homework. He was persuasive in helping senior management to feel comfortable with his ability to do the work. He got the job. ❑

Career Change

You may be different from Malcolm. Suppose you want to change careers and do something different. A friend of ours recently changed from an investment banking position to the chief financial officer of a small bio-tech firm. Even in a major change such as this one some of your skills are directly applicable (finance in this case). So let's say that you are looking at a function that would use 20 to 30 percent of your prior experience and that would be 70 to 80 percent new. First, you need to defend your ability to perform the 20 to 30 percent by citing pertinent accomplishments in that arena. The 70 to 80 percent of the new job responsibility represents an opportunity to sell the interviewer on your potential. You have to persuade the interviewer that the skills you have

attained throughout your business career and life can assist you in performing the job successfully. Changes like this usually occur when the
interviewer with the hiring authority "falls in love" with the applicant
and feels that the applicant could work effectively and successfully with
him to accomplish the goals of the business. I (Fred) made this type of
change a number of years ago.

CAREER PROFILE
Skill Match

I had been the assistant superintendent for personnel in a large,
heterogeneous school system. I was the school board's professional witness in legal matters in addition to labor negotiations,
employment, employee relations, and training and development
functions.

I was being considered for a human resources consulting assignment in the private sector that involved new business development, counseling, and administration. You can imagine the
issue. I had to help the partners and senior consultants understand the skills that I had developed and that could help me become successful in a new environment. For example, I indicated:

"I developed an ability to interact with people from every background and socioeconomic level."

"I assisted opposing sides to develop realistic positions in resolving disputes."

"I developed strong negotiating skills."

"I developed the ability to be persuasive under pressure (as the
professional witness in legal proceedings)."

"I helped individuals solve problems."

Then I had to back up my statements with specific examples
with great detail. After several interviews, the partners became
comfortable that my organization had many similarities to their
own and that the skills I had developed could help me to be successful in the private sector.

I had prepared well. Because I was changing careers, however, it took a series of interviews with almost every partner and
senior consultant. As time went on, the organization became
more and more comfortable with me and I was eventually offered a position.   ❏

First Position

The approach is much the same if you are entering the job market for the first time: Concentrate on your prior accomplishments and potential. You may not have experience but you have a lot of abilities that organizations need to maintain a vitality, such as energy, potential, and excitement, as well as inquisitiveness, creativity, a new point of view. These are all things that are vital to any organization. Make sure that you talk about these assets in an interview. What can you add to your own list?

CAREER PROFILE
Related Experiences

Steve had recently completed law school and was interviewing for a position in a suburban law firm. He knew that selling new business would be a critical issue in the interview since he was not in a position to bring business with him. He analyzed his skills and was prepared to talk about his ability to establish rapport, listen, communicate, consult, persuade, and present. But he knew they would not be as important as his ability to sell new business. He identified some of his key lifetime accomplishments that dealt with sales, such as:

1. The leading Boy Scout three years in a row in a fund raising drive.

2. President of the student government elected in a close, competitive election.

3. An entrepreneur who purchased old milk cans, painted them in a colonial motif, and sold them at a roadside stand to make money for college.

4. The Key Club member selected by his college to meet potential incoming students and "sell" them on his university.

Steve made an excellent presentation of how his skills and accomplishments gave evidence of his potential to sell legal services. Steve's potential employer became his new employer.   ❏

We have to make a point about the enthusiasm of youth. Don't underestimate the power of this characteristic. Sell the fact that you have always been a positive person with lots of energy and drive. Bob, a personal friend, is president and CEO of his own business. He tells the story of hiring two young engineers for his environmental (air and water) company.

Within a few weeks, the engineering department emanated an enthusi-asm and sense of fun that Bob hadn't seen in a number of years. When Bob told us the story, his eyes sparkled, and it was obvious that he was excit-ed about what was happening.

Summary

An important aspect of intellectual preparation is career assessment, which covers where you have been in your career, where you are now, and where you are going. Specifically:

- Examine why you are interested in a new position.
- Define your key competencies.
- List five accomplishments to defend each competency (including how each affected the bottom line).
- Define your ideal company, job, and boss.

PART 3

Finesse the Interview

Know the Interviewer's Agenda

The next two chapters are concerned with understanding the roles of the interviewer and the candidate. This chapter examines the interview from the interviewer's point of view; the next looks at it from the candidate's point of view. In the same way that an excellent negotiator should be able to represent either side, an outstanding candidate should understand what the interviewer is trying to accomplish and why. Greater knowledge of each role prepares you for any eventuality and prevents surprises, the scourge of any candidate. In addition, understanding the interviewer's agenda helps you with one of your most important tasks: helping interviewers accomplish their agendas.

The goals of the hiring process are to fill an open position and, in the long term, to raise the overall ability level of the staff. Although these are the stated goals, all sorts of human variables intervene to make the decision more subjective and less technical or skill-oriented. To offset this tendency, hiring theory suggests that an organization should establish an interview team rather than a single interviewer to accomplish the process.

Keeping It Simple

Although each interviewer brings individual needs and a particular style to the table, there are some generally accepted notions on conducting interviews. You should understand these notions, as well as the flow of information in an interview and some of the terms you will hear, such as screening interviewers, hiring interviewers, job specifications, professional characteristics, and personal characteristics.

To keep the discussion simple, we prefer to separate the interviewers into screening interviewers and hiring interviewers. *Screening interviewers* can eliminate a candidate from further progress, but cannot hire. *Hiring interviewers* either have individual hiring authority or are part of an interviewing team with that authority.

Screening interviewers are usually human resource professionals, search consultants, or specialists of other kinds. Their function is to determine whether you have the skills to do the job and the potential to be a good fit within the company.

Hiring interviewers are usually some combination of direct boss, senior managers, and others with direct knowledge of the position. Their function is to find the best candidate from among those the screeners endorse.

Job specifications (or *specs*) include job title, duties, reporting relationship, mandatory educational or other requirements, and approximate compensation, together with the professional and personal characteristics necessary to be successful. Hiring theory suggests that some combination of screening and hiring interviewers meet to define the characteristics of the ideal candidate.

Professional characteristics are usually fairly easy to identify. They are defined in terms of educational background, professional credentials, and business expertise. The general statement of a job title might be "Manager of Internal Audit." More specific requirements might be "experience in a manufacturing company" or "auditing management experience preferred." Very specific requirements might be "CPA," "minimum of two years in public accounting," or "five years experience managing a department of 10 or more people."

Personal characteristics are less clearly understood and often not identified. They are defined in terms of interpersonal skills, management style, attitudes, and values. Since successful job performance is often associated with personal skills, it is worthwhile to try to describe the culture and the characteristics that make the employee a "fit" in that company. "Aggressive, individualistic, bottom-line-oriented," or "team-oriented, consensus builder, goal-directed" might be a start to defining success in a given company.

Because completed job specifications often describe someone who can walk on water, it's important for the organization to think in terms of "must have" characteristics versus "desirable" but not absolutely necessary characteristics.

INTERVIEW TIP—SCHEDULING

Leave plenty of time at both ends of the interview so that you arrive early and can remain late. This reduces stress and shows interest.

With the job specification in place and a strong concept of the kind of person the organization wants, the screening interviewers can begin to identify potential candidates. The interviewers are normally search consultants, if the position has been put out to search, or human resource professionals, if the search is conducted by in-house staff.

(*Note:* A number of interview tips are offered in the pages ahead. They are particularly intended for recent college graduates who may be new to the interview process and those who have not interviewed recently. They are listed in Appendix A for review prior to an interview.)

CAREER PROFILE
The First Encounter

An assessment of personal skills begins the minute someone from the organization first lays eyes on the candidate. This may or may not be the interviewer. It might be a receptionist or secretary. Initial impressions are extremely important.

Nicholas knew that he had made a mistake the minute he left home. He was leaving 20 minutes later than he wanted due to a personal problem at home. The 20 minutes compounded his problem by throwing him into rush hour traffic. By the time he drove in the company gates he was already 10 minutes late.

The first person Nicholas saw was Sam, a security guard. Nicholas was beside himself with the stress of the commute and the fact he was late. He got out of the car and literally sprinted over to Sam to get directions to the correct building. Nicholas was abrupt and to the point. Sam tried to be helpful, but his learning disability kept him from processing the request for information as quickly as Nicholas wanted and needed it. Nicholas was visibly disturbed, making Sam's task all the more difficult. Finally, Nicholas obtained the information and raced on.

Nicholas found Meredith, Mr. Aldrich's executive secretary. When he discovered that Mr. Aldrich was running late and had not yet arrived, Nicholas' perception of the situation improved

---

INTERVIEW TIP—CONGENIAL ATTITUDE

Treat every person you meet as if he were the CEO. He might have a direct connection to the CEO or even be the CEO himself.

---

dramatically. He began to relax and got a grip on himself. While he chatted with Meredith, he discovered that they both rooted for the same baseball team, and they had a great time predicting trades and second-guessing the manager. By the time Mr. Aldrich arrived, Nicholas was relaxed and confident. They had a terrific meeting. There was strong rapport and Nicholas liked everything he heard about the manner in which the organization handled its people. One big happy family. Mutual respect for everyone. Nicholas left the meeting feeling confident; Mr. Aldrich had said he would be called back to meet other key players in the firm.

That night at the dinner table, Meredith told her family, who were also baseball fanatics, about the candidate she had met at work that day who knew so much about baseball. As she described Nicholas, Sam, her brother, became more and more uncomfortable. He lowered his head. When Meredith noticed he had withdrawn from the conversation she asked, "Sam, are you okay?" Sam wouldn't speak for a few minutes.

When he said, "I don't like that man. He was mean to me. He scared me," Meredith was amazed. She questioned her brother, gathering all the details of his encounter with Nicholas. Meredith knew that Sam liked everyone. Surely if he had such a strong reaction there must have been something in Nicholas that she had missed. Something worth thinking about.

When Meredith went to work the next day she told Mr. Aldrich the whole story. He listened carefully and at the conclusion restated to Meredith the importance that he placed on interpersonal concern and caring within the firm.

Nicholas never received a call back. He waited a few weeks and started calling. Mr. Aldrich did not receive his calls. Finally, Nicholas called late one day and Mr. Aldrich answered the telephone. He was short and cold. "The job has been filled," he said. As Nicholas hung up, he was stunned. His last meeting had been great. Now this. Nicholas never knew what hit him. And he never dreamed that his encounter with the security guard was his undoing. ❑

The "Normalcy" Test

Interviewers play Solomon. On the one hand, they want to give candidates an opportunity to sell themselves, while on the other, they need to fill the position with the best person they can identify within the time constraints. Hence, screening interviewers need to eliminate candidates and pare down the list, and hiring interviewers need to make the selection. To accomplish the task quickly and efficiently, balancing tests and scoring systems are devised.

Most interviewers engage in their own personal "normalcy" test. We say their own test because there is no one style or format. In most cases it begins right at the start of the interview, is informal and conversational in tone, and is broad and general rather than specific. The test is part of, and impossible to distinguish from, the rapport building that two people do at the beginning of an interview.

The nonverbal portion is an opportunity for the interviewer to observe the candidate. The interviewer seeks data concerning overall personality, dress, fitness, demeanor, and mannerisms. A series of mental questions helps the interviewer keep track of the data required.

- Does the candidate make a good appearance?
- Is her dress appropriate?
- Does she appear confident and friendly?
- Does she smile?
- How does she carry herself?
- Does she have any unusual mannerisms?

Interviewers are looking for deviations from their concept of ideal behavior for someone at the level of the open position. Tim, who has just graduated from college would not be expected to have the same quality of dress as Susan, a proven senior executive. However, Tim would be expected to have on a conservative, dark suit and tie if that's the company culture.

The verbal portion of the "normalcy" test begins during the "get to know you" or rapport building mode. The purpose is the same as in the nonverbal check: Does the interviewer find differences between actual and expected behavior? Rapport building is a critical time for both the interviewer and the candidate. The introductory period lasts as long as the interviewer feels it is productive or time constraints allow. Most theory indicates that an interviewer discovers a lot about a job seeker, including attitudes, values, behavior, and management style by helping the individual to relax and become comfortable.

Consequently, most interviewers spend time focusing on the candidate's personal interests or mutual interests. This time normally gives the candidate a chance to relax and become comfortable in the new surroundings.

Suppose, for example, the interviewer and Kristina were having a conversation about skiing.

> INTERVIEWER: Kristina, I see that you have an interest in skiing.
>
> KRISTINA: Yes. I really enjoy skiing.
>
> INTERVIEWER: Have you been interested in skiing for long?
>
> KRISTINA: All my life. My father was on the United States downhill ski team, and he started my brother and me on skis at the age of three.
>
> INTERVIEWER: Have you skied competitively?
>
> KRISTINA: Yes, I have won numerous championships, but unfortunately there isn't enough money in the sport to make it a full-time occupation.
>
> INTERVIEWER: You seem a little sad about that.
>
> KRISTINA: Well, I guess I am. It has been a big part of my life.
>
> INTERVIEWER: Are you able to keep up with your skiing now that you've graduated and have been working full-time?
>
> KRISTINA: Absolutely. I go to Vermont every weekend from October to March or April.

Those are simple enough statements: "unfortunately there isn't enough money … to make it a full-time occupation" and "I go to Vermont every weekend from October to March or April." They seem to be speaking, however, about big time commitments. Kristina didn't say, "a few weekends" or "a number of weekends" or even "most weekends." She made it clear that it was "every weekend." Now there is an issue to be addressed on the interviewer's normalcy balancing scale. Has the interest gone past "normal" or "reasonable" and into a red flag zone?

On the one hand, Kristina has every right to her personal life, interests, and passions. Passions may even indicate energy, excitement, and zest for life. Indeed, many employers look for employees who have participated in competitive sports because they know about dedication, commitment, and how to win.

On the other hand, what about the company and its needs? If hired, will Kristina come to work on Mondays and Fridays with enthusiasm for her job? Or will those days be mental extensions of her weekend? What happens when there is an emergency project that requires evening or weekend work? How about the two corporate planning weekends that occur each year between October and April?

How the interviewer weighs that short dialog may well be the critical determinant in whether Kristina's candidacy continues or ends. The normalcy

---

INTERVIEW TIP—DRESS

Your dress should be appropriate and on the conservative side for the company (and industry).

---

test continues just as it did in our example throughout the interview, with the interviewer making value judgments that reject or propel a candidacy.

At the conclusion of the initial "get to know you" time, the interviewer normally throws a signal to indicate that it is time to move on. It can be framed in many different ways. For example:

Would you tell me about your career path?

I've enjoyed getting to know you, and now I need to ask you some questions.

I'd like to ask you about your business career.

If there is no clear signal, the emphasis shifts to business-oriented questions. The candidate must remember, however, that rapport building and the "normalcy" test continue throughout the interview.

The interviewer needs to address a series of areas during the interview. Good business practice has taught interviewers to be subtle in their approach rather than blunt. Interviewers rarely ask, for instance:

You look a little slow moving. Will you be able to demonstrate the high level of energy that this job will require?

You seem a little high-strung. How do you think you will react under the day-to-day stress we have here?

You seem extremely aggressive. How do you think you will be able to interact with our more laid-back clients?

More often than not, interviewers use finesse, asking questions about personal background, level of education, and career history, including specific case studies, strengths and weaknesses, and outside interests to gather the data needed. The information generally fits into two categories: personal and professional characteristics.

Personal Characteristics

Personal characteristics give evidence that the candidate's interpersonal skills, management style, attitudes, and values are consistent with others in the organization. The areas of concern to the interviewer are:

- Interpersonal skills.
- Style.
- Attitudes and values.
- Motivation.
- Outside interests.

Interpersonal Skills

While the interviewer could attempt to observe many individual skills, she normally limits herself to the interaction of a few critical ones.

1. She wants to get a feel for the candidate's general understanding of human behavior: What makes other people tick.
2. Next, she wants to discover the candidate's understanding of tact and diplomacy or politics, as well as his understanding of reading between the lines and understanding hidden agendas.
3. Finally, she'll look to evaluate the candidate's empathy level or the ability and willingness to take the time to understand and deal with the underlying motivations of others.

The interaction of these three skill clusters is of real interest to the interviewer. What may be good in one situation may be less appropriate or even bad in another. Someone who is strong in all three areas may be an excellent candidate to work in a highly political organization where politics is as important, or perhaps more important, to getting ahead as productivity. Other individuals who have a strong task orientation may score high on general understanding of human behavior but low on tact and diplomacy and low on empathy. This does not mean that they don't care about other people or their problems, but their desire to complete the task successfully is so overriding that it supersedes the time and effort that tact and empathy require.

The interviewer usually presents different scenarios of possible interactions at the appropriate level for the candidate and then determines whether you have to think very hard about your response. She evaluates the strength of your answer. The interviewer's evaluation goes beyond a generic rating to a function-specific examination. In this regard, individuals who are in sales almost always must be viewed as having high levels of empathy to function effectively.

For the executive, on the other hand, high levels of empathy may not be viewed as positive. While there needs to be a balance in terms of empathic response to others, too low a score indicates a task motivation or task orientation that could interfere with effective management techniques. Too high a score can indicate that the individual may be too concerned with or sensitive to the underlying motivations of others and therefore will not be as effective in getting the job done. In fact, when compared with successful executives, high-empathy people are likely to be described as too soft or too concerned about other people's feelings to get the task accomplished.

Style

Style is the combination of temperament, interpersonal skills, and understanding as well as intellect and problem solving approaches. The issue for the interviewer is to determine how these skills will come together in a working or management style. On the personal side, for example, the interviewer needs to know if you are aggressive or laid back, outgoing or introverted, flexible or rigid, direct or circuitous, and scheduled or spontaneous. On the professional side the issues might be whether you prefer autocratic or participative decision making, a team-oriented or individualistic work atmosphere, an intuitive or logical approach to problem solving, and a strong concern for the logic of a decision or the impact of that decision on people.

The best way to obtain data regarding style is first-hand observation. This method is often impossible, but the interviewer may be able to talk to former superiors or subordinates in addition to the candidate. The interviewer typically discusses actual case studies with you to gather information. A wise interviewer discusses how and why you made decisions and how you interacted with superiors, peers, and subordinates because it is common for individuals to exhibit different styles when working with different levels within the organization.

Another variable in style is stress. People behave differently under varying degrees of stress. A few interviewers still like "stress interviews," which are designed to put a person under considerable tension and push them to behave in ways that would only occur in high-pressure situations. This is not a particularly well regarded hiring technique today, but clearly it has been used in the past. All people going through a selection interview are likely to experience some levels of stress (usually self-generated).

Perhaps the most important consideration relating to style is not what the candidate does, but rather what the company itself has done. The organization needs to examine itself and determine the style that has proven most effective in moving the business forward. You would be surprised at how many times the interviewing team is either not in agreement or clearly has an incorrect perception of successful style in their own organization.

Another variable is management edict. A senior executive can say, "We need a hard-nosed, no-nonsense, take-charge kind of individual. I'm sick and tired of not getting results and having no one accepting responsibility for the failure." What typically happens is that the interview team finds that type of person whose style is tough, autocratic, and individualistic. What the senior executive, in his momentary frustration, forgot to realize is that the organization was built on teamwork and participative management. This is obviously not fair to the executive or to the organization.

Attitudes and Values

Many interviewers feel that *attitudes and values* are the most important areas aside from skills. These are an individual's beliefs about other people, about the world, about the business; they are the values that individuals bring to a job on both a personal and interpersonal level. They dictate how they are likely to interact with others and their effectiveness in present or potential management roles. If your attitudes and values match the organization's, then there is likely to be a good fit.

The interviewer's concern is to go beyond the basics to understand what attitudes and values drive the candidate. How strongly, for example, does the candidate value family and time with the family? Are the activities that support the family unit important, such as coach, church volunteer, scout leader? At work, it is not just "does the candidate like work," but issues such as "how does he value his relationships with people?" Is the candidate, for example, used to spending time with people at work and socializing with people from the organization on the weekends? What is the candidate's attitude toward quality work? The range extends from "get the product out the door, even if there are returns," to "meet the deadline," to "the product will leave only when it is perfect, regardless of time constraints." Where does the candidate stand on the issue of personal achievement versus organizational achievement? A candidate with a strong personal achievement orientation typically has a very difficult time in a company that values organizational achievement above personal achievement.

These are a few of the many issues that are probably important to the interviewer. The list depends on the environment of the organization. Other possibilities include:

- What is the candidate's attitude toward the relationship of management and labor?

- How does the candidate like to be managed?

- What recognition and approach does the candidate have toward internal politics?

CAREER PROFILE
Family Values

Candidates (and interviewers) often don't recognize the importance of attitudes and values until it stares them right in the face. Kevin had been a contributing member of his very aggressive organization for about ten years. He had worked hard and been successful both from an interpersonal and a productivity point of view. Kevin had been promoted in accord with his productivity. His reputation had spread to other divisions of the company.

Kevin was also known in the company as being a strong family man and a pillar of his community. He had a wife and two children, and he served on a number of community boards that supported activities of interest to members of his family.

One day he received a call from a close friend in another division of the company telling him of an opening in his department and asking Kevin if he had any interest. It represented a whopping promotion. Kevin was stunned but he indicated a definite interest. His friend, David, indicated that he was not the only candidate and that he would have to interview for the position. That did not bother Kevin and he accepted. Kevin knew that David was aware of his strengths; he was sure he would be a good candidate.

The interview went smoothly in a conversational style. There was no need for David to probe too deeply because he knew Kevin so well. The crux of the conversation came down to the following dialog:

> DAVID: Kevin, there is only one concern I have about your candidacy—your ability to balance work and the affairs of your personal life.
>
> KEVIN: Why is that a concern, David? You know that I work hard and am always willing to do extra for the organization.
>
> DAVID: What about weekend work?
>
> KEVIN: I don't have a problem with coming in once in a while on the weekend.
>
> DAVID: How old are your children now?
>
> KEVIN: Thirteen and nine.
>
> DAVID: That is very important, and those are very impressionable ages.
>
> KEVIN: I agree; what is your point?
>
> DAVID: In your present responsibility don't you normally leave on the 5:30 P.M. train to go home?

KEVIN: Yes, but as I indicated, I am willing to stay late when work calls.

DAVID: Listen to me. You are a great candidate for this job and, if you want it, I will hire you. But you need to recognize and focus on the fact that your family life is going to change radically if you take this job. You will not leave on the 5:30 P.M. train. It will much more likely be the 8:30 P.M. train or later. All the time. And you will work on the weekend on a much more regular basis. Not every weekend but two or three per month. Have you discussed this with your wife and family?

KEVIN: No, I haven't. You're right, David. I need to think about that issue. Thanks.

Ultimately, Kevin did not take the job. After discussions with his wife and family, he called David back and declined. His attitudes and values placed a higher worth on time with his family than on a large promotion including a great deal more money. David was an interviewer who knew and understood the culture of his organization better than most and was kind enough to make Kevin focus on the key issue.   ❑

Motivation

Motivation can be somewhat difficult to identify in the selection process. The interviewer really has to dig into the candidate's past history and get examples of actions taken, successes, failures, and what was important about a given situation that led to success or failure. The interviewer knows that more proof is needed than candidates' stating they are highly motivated. The interviewer is trying to determine whether money, success, achievement, or the opportunity to work in a creative mode, for example, is the candidate's principal motivation.

It is also important for the interviewer to determine how motivated candidates are by one of the many social reinforcers. If, for example, an individual is strongly motivated by positive regard, recognition, and pats on the back, then money alone may not be a sufficient reward to keep motivation levels high. In this situation a team-oriented environment is an important ingredient in the success quotient. If, on the other hand, the components that are most important in the motivational picture are an opportunity to work in a creative mode or personal achievement, then these need to be taken into consideration in assessing a person's suitability for a particular position.

Many successful salespeople, for example, are not really highly motivated by the interpersonal interaction side of the equation. Rather, they have very short reinforcement links. In other words, they need immediate reinforcement for their actions, and frequently the best measure of success is the number of dollars that they can accrue over a short period of time. For this kind of individual, motivation needs to be focused around how they can, in fact, generate more dollars in a short amount of time rather than "how great it's going to be to interact with the guys."

CAREER PROFILE
Fire in the Belly

A piece of the motivation picture is energy, and the interviewer is always looking for evidence to indicate whether this is a problem. (*Note:* Energy is an attitudinal variable, not age-related.) Jim had been the head of the six-person legal department of a $4 billion midwestern firm. He had built the department from nothing to its present level. He had been highly successful but found himself out of work, along with the rest of his department, when the company was sold.

Jim was nervous about his age and the fact that he had not interviewed for some time. He was in his mid-50s. His first interview was for a position similar to his former one. Jim answered all the questions regarding education and work history with enthusiasm and poise. He was extremely positive when talking about building and managing a legal department, and he was specific about how he had recruited an attorney who functioned in a highly specialized discipline. He told the interviewer the number of hours per week he averaged at work and demonstrated a knowledge of creative solutions to difficult problems. In addition, his demeanor was very confident and upbeat which, together with his answers, was viewed positively by the interviewer. All indications were that Jim was a candidate with high motivation and energy level.

Some time later the interviewer moved to a new subject, outside interests. She asked, "What civic or social activities do you most enjoy?" Jim had resisted doing much preparation in the area of his outside interests. His response was, "I really haven't been involved in any because I have been working so hard that when I come home I am exhausted." The second that Jim uttered the words he knew that he had made a huge mistake. He did his best to further explain what he meant but it was like a newspaper retraction a week later. The damage was done.

To make matters worse, Jim had given two wrong signals. First, he had been involved in civic activities. His lack of preparation prevented him from remembering which activities. Second, his statement about exhaustion was overstated because he had been surprised and reacted poorly. Jim had periods of fatigue, like the rest of us, when there were emergency projects or activities that took inordinate amounts of time. Exhausted, however, was not his normal state of being. Jim never forgot the lessons he learned from this interviewing experience and he subsequently landed a new position quickly.   ❏

Demonstrating energy is a key factor for an entry-level candidate as well. Entry-level candidates do not have loads of experience; so they must sell enthusiasm, motivation, and energy. From the interviewer's point of view, if entry-level candidates, with little or no experience, don't bring energy, enthusiasm, and motivation to the organization, then why hire them?

Outside Interests

Outside interests are of concern to the interviewer because they give information about style, values, and motivation as well as showing breadth of interests. They also give the interviewer an idea of how candidates are likely to use their time and whether or not they are going to be well balanced with respect to work versus play.

Certainly there is a need to find someone who will work hard, but there is also the desire for a colleague who is interesting and fun to be around. Someone with whom folks would like to spend time outside of work. Someone with a sense of humor. In addition, there is mounting evidence that indicates working extremely long hours, day after day, leads to a loss of efficiency in the workplace. So balance matters a great deal to the interviewer.

Many organizations also want leaders and potential leaders to be involved in the community. First, volunteerism reflects well on the company with its people giving something back to the community. Second, it may teach new and important skills to executives, rising stars, and future leaders. The need for cultural diversity is today's reality and will continue to expand in the 21st century. Community service is a laboratory for a candidate to learn the skills of managing individuals who come from diverse backgrounds. Add to this the issue of motivating volunteers whose agendas sometimes differ from the stated goals of the organization. Many people believe that these are among the most difficult of management assignments and consequently teach many valuable skills.

CAREER PROFILE
Volunteer Work

In addition, community service can sometimes be turned into a significant advantage in the workplace. Susan had been a captain in her local United Way for a number of years. Her work gave her a great sense of pride and satisfaction. When it came time for her to look for a new job, she was asked if she had supervisory experience. She responded, "Yes, I have been a captain in the United Way for the last eight years." Not only did that experience put her in a different category than the other candidates, but her potential boss was also a United Way volunteer. Susan won the job.   ❏

Professional Characteristics

Professional characteristics give evidence of the candidate's educational background, professional credentials, and business experience that provides the background for successful performance. Communication, leadership/management abilities, and organizational fit offer information concerning your ability to fit comfortably within the organizational setting and to produce. The areas of concern to the interviewer are:

- Intelligence/technical skills.
- Experience.
- Communication.
- Leadership/management abilities.
- Organizational fit.

Intelligence/Technical Skills

Intelligence is one measure of potential job success. Since intelligence can be defined in many ways depending on your point of view, interviewers look for as many objective hooks as possible to defend their evaluation. High school grades, SAT scores, college attended, college grades, graduate school attended, graduate school grades are all examples that give evidence of intelligence.

The college and course of study are most important to the interviewer when it is the candidate's first job. The stronger the college program is, the more it can be used as evidence of intelligence and the fewer questions the interviewer needs to ask. Interviewers also know, however, that students choose colleges for a variety of reasons, many of which are beyond their control. Examples are cost, proximity to home, or restrictions imposed by parents. The interviewer wants to probe these issues to understand high school interests, the college selection process, the major and why it was selected, the degree of enjoyment and satisfaction with the major, and grades in and out of the major for each college attended.

The interviewer also likes to be able to quantify the candidate's technical skills via a professional degree and/or license from a highly accredited school. An engineering degree from Purdue University with a 3.5 average is a strong indicator that the candidate has the necessary technical skills to perform. Interviewers may also want to delve into the specifics of the program. Many highly recognized schools throughout the country give MBA's. Some are general in nature, some specialize in marketing or finance, and some are heavily quantitative. The job specification may call for an emphasis in one area or another.

CAREER PROFILE
Following Interests

Another means for the interviewer to gain evidence of intelligence and technical skills is to follow interests to see where they lead. Richard didn't want to attend college after graduating from high school. He got a job as an automobile mechanic working on sophisticated foreign sports cars and quickly received a number of promotions until he became the service manager of the dealership at the age of 20. He was probably the youngest service manager in the country. His interests also turned to servicing airplane engines, and he attained a pilot's license. Then, at the age of 22, he decided to go back to college. He earned an engineering degree and now develops sophisticated financial products on Wall Street.   ❏

The savvy interviewer will understand what it takes to be successful in his industry, company, and job function. It isn't always possible to quantify intelligence and technical skills because everyone doesn't need credentials (such as an MBA, Ph.D., M.D., D.D.S.). Consequently, the interviewer may need to follow the candidate's progress as she did Richard's to tell whether there are strong sales skills, merchandising skills, finance skills, or whatever additional skill base is required.

Experience

Job experience and career direction are of great interest to the interviewer. Why a candidate selected a career path can give many signals about interests and aptitude. With a recent graduate, career direction has to be the focus of the interviewer. With an experienced candidate, the interviewer wants to understand the motivation for taking and leaving each job, and carefully evaluates whether the career is progressing in a steadily upward direction. With the recent trends to remove layers of middle management, there are more lateral moves than in the past. The interviewer wants to understand the challenges in each job; otherwise, a lateral move could be perceived as a negative.

As the interviewer tries to understand the career overview, those candidates who have more predictable career paths (such as assistant product manager to product manager to group product manager) are easier to understand. If the candidate has had a successful stint with a well established, blue chip firm such as a Procter & Gamble, that gives the interviewer greater confidence in his abilities. The interviewer can then focus on variables like the actual time to promotion versus the expected time to promotion.

When the candidate is from the same industry, the interviewer can compare accomplishments directly. Suppose, however, an organization wanted someone from another industry, but needed someone who had experience making rapid fire, clear decisions. As an example, a candidate who has successfully managed an airport should have an easy time convincing an interviewer in this regard.

The more diversified the experience, the more candidates may have to help interviewers understand how their skills and abilities are appropriate to the job. For example, the candidate for the talk show host has to sell the interviewer on his interviewing and persuasive skills, which were developed while previously employed as a TV evangelist, consumer products salesperson, or school board member. A recent graduate or a career changer is judged on potential. Lifetime skills and accomplishments become important in these situations because of their general nature.

With the overview clear in her mind, the interviewer's questions usually start with the "what," "when," and "where" questions. Although the questions may be asked in interesting or creative ways the underlying intent is to get at:

- "What did you do?"
- "When did you do it?"
- "Where did you do it?"

Depending on the direction set by the interviewer, a greater or lesser degree of detail is requested for each job. As the interviewer senses an important point in the candidate's career or one that she thinks is important to the new position, the questioning usually becomes more complex and includes the "how" and "why" questions. These questions are designed to examine interpersonal skills, attitudes and values, and management style, and they give the interviewer clues regarding organizational fit. To kick off the questioning, the interviewer might ask:

- "Why did you decide to reorganize your department?"
- "How did you implement the decision?"
- "What was the impact on the professional staff?"
- "How did the decision impact net profits?"

This might then lead to a full discussion of a job assignment, project, or problem that needed to be solved with an entire series of how and why questions. The interviewer typically spends a good deal of the interview time talking about your experiences and asking how you might handle given situations. The interviewer is able to gather a great deal of information about all the characteristics we are discussing from your answers to the questions.

Communication

Communication skills are one of the few characteristics that the interviewer can observe first-hand. Since each person in an organization must be a salesperson for ideas, products, or services, communication skills are vital.

CAREER PROFILE
Unprofessional Behavior

The interview should have been merely a formality. Mike, a bright young administrator was one of two finalists for a promotion in a large suburban hospital with a national reputation for excellence. He was the candidate from inside the organization for the position, and his track record had been impressive during the four years he'd been employed there. He was respected and popular, known both for his ability to get the job done and for his warm, easy manner. The hospital administrator liked him very much; in fact, he had hired Mike originally and continued to be impressed with him.

Mike knew a group of his colleagues would be among the interviewers, and he more or less knew the questions. He was even familiar with the board conference room where the interviewing would take place. Nothing should go wrong. But his interview blew him out of the water and out of contention for the promotion. And he had no one to blame but himself.

When the administrator brought Mike into the interview and began to introduce him to the group, Mike smiled and interrupted the administrator, "I think I already know everybody." He looked around the group, waved his hand, and breezily said, "Hi, guys." As he sat down, he pushed his chair away from the table a bit and leaned back, crossing his legs. Throughout the 45-minute interview he frequently made joking, sarcastic remarks. To be conversational he used phrases like "a hell of a good idea" and "a damn fine plan." Once, when he didn't have a ready response, he allowed, "I don't want to BS you by making up an answer."

Mike interrupted two different interviewers when he thought he understood their line of questioning and in response to one question about crisis management, he chuckled and responded, "Well, you know, it can be a zoo around here at certain times." Toward the end of the interview, the administrator asked Mike if he had any questions of the group. "Nope," he replied, "I pretty much know everything I need to know about the position and the hospital."

The group was polite in thanking Mike for meeting them, but when he left the room, there was total silence. Finally, the chairman of the hospital's board of trustees spoke to the hospital administrator. "I know you're really high on Mike's abilities," he said, "and I respect your judgment. I also am willing to admit that what we just witnessed might not be a true indication of who Mike really is and what he can do, but whether this was a fluke or not, it happened. Mike was unprofessional and inappropriate during this interview, and we can't run the risk of having him be unprofessional when he represents this hospital. Despite the fact that I like Mike personally, I cannot vote to promote him." The rest of the group quickly agreed and Mike lost his opportunity to advance.

First and foremost, the interview team was conducting a formal business meeting, which demanded a formal, businesslike manner. They were expecting to see a relaxed and confident, but totally professional Mike and certainly not the informal side of him that might be found on the golf course or at a party with close friends.

The team expected Mike to greet each person with a smile and a handshake and for him to sit in a relaxed but alert position. They expected him to listen closely to a question in its entirety and to answer concisely. Good eye contact with each member of

---

INTERVIEW TIP—POSITIVE COMMENTS

Speak only positively about your company (or former company) and the people in the organization—there is no room in an interview for disparaging remarks, however lighthearted their intent.

---

the team was expected over the course of the interview with specific eye contact given to the interviewer who asked the last question. Mike was expected to speak clearly. Since most people speed up their rate of speaking when they're nervous, it was important for Mike to be aware that the pace might need to be slowed a bit.

Furthermore, the interview team expected Mike to be organized, specific, and logical in his delivery. They would not have been concerned if Mike had been silent for several seconds to consider a question and prepare his answer. That behavior, however, would not have been acceptable had Mike taken time before every answer. Then it might have been taken as a sign that he was unsure or unprepared.

Finally, the team had some very specific "don'ts" in interviewing.

- *Don't ever interrupt.* The interviewer is in charge. If he wants to interrupt a candidate, it is his prerogative to do so and the candidate should let him. If a question is too long or involved, the candidate can always ask for clarification to be certain he understood the question.

- *Don't use slang* or even mild cursing; neither is professional.

- *Don't use sarcastic humor.* It's never certain how it will be interpreted.

- *Don't ever put down a current boss or company.*

- *Don't pass up the opportunity to ask a question.* Intelligent, thoughtful questions can show grasp of a situation or the research that's been done to prepare for the interview.   ❏

Leadership/Management Abilities

Leadership is defined as "showing the way by going in front of ..." or "one who starts something...." *Management* is defined as, "the skillful handling of people and details so as to get results ..." or "supervising the action of a group working together...." In today's world where small, quick, action-oriented teams or individuals make decisions at lower and lower levels in the organization, leadership skills are clearly more necessary than ever. Leadership is one of those nebulous qualities that drives interviewers crazy. The CEO of a major consumer products company once told us, "I don't know how to define it, or tell if a candidate has it, but I sure know leadership when I see it exhibited in a business setting." Analogies such as "the leader knows where to place the ladder" and "the manager knows how to climb the ladder" abound in professional literature.

It is also clear, however, that with less middle management and other administrative support, corporate teams must possess a blend of leadership and management skills. It is not enough to devise creative solutions to problems; the team must also be able to implement the program effectively. Comparisons between leadership skills and management skills can be identified as the following continuums:

Leader	*Manager*
Conceptualizes	Analyzes
Envisions/inspires	Plans/implements the game plan
Takes risks	Solves problems
Produces change	Produces order
Relies on people	Relies on systems

At times, the interviewer needs to fill a position that is heavily focused on leadership skills or management skills. In other cases, the position may require both types of skills, as in the following case study. In this situation the interviewer wants to understand the skills the candidate has developed.

CAREER PROFILE
Leadership and Management

Marian was the superintendent of schools in a system with two large high schools. One was regarded as more desirable by the better educated, more articulate parents, but was overcrowded. The less desirable school had abundant space. Marian explained to the community the process she followed in gathering data in order to redistrict the school system. She also explained all the steps she followed in public awareness and input. Plans were formulated, following all the steps that logic would dictate. (Note the management skills.) However, the issue was more emotional than logical. At this point she had no choice. Marian made the decision to redistrict some students, recommended it, and the school board approved her recommendation. (Note the leadership skills.)

INTERVIEW TIP—PREPARATION

Be prepared to give examples of your leadership and management abilities in your personal as well as your business life.

It was an extremely unpopular decision with those who felt that they were negatively affected.

It would have been easy for Marian to move on to other pressing issues. Instead, she met with the press and spoke on local cable TV stations to explain the reasons for the changes. (Note the leadership skills.) She made sure that nothing fell between the cracks. Orientation sessions for the redistricted students made them feel more comfortable. In addition, faculty of both schools met with parents. In short, she did everything possible to provide a smooth transition. (Note the management skills.) Despite her best efforts a small group of parents chose to file suit. One year later, after litigation, Marian's position had been 100 percent upheld from a legal and policy standpoint by the State Commissioner of Education. Marian's case study demonstrated her ability to plan as a manager and presented an excellent example of her leadership abilities.   ❏

Leadership and management potential can be assessed in the same manner. It isn't acceptable for the candidate to say, for example, that he hasn't yet had the opportunity to assume a leadership position. Instead of focusing on work experiences, an outstanding interviewer focuses on the nonwork experiences, which include athletics, school experiences, and personal life.

Suppose, for example, the candidate was discussing his interest in children's theater and how he had directed plays involving 15 volunteers from the theater guild, over 30 child actors, and 60 parents of those children. The discussion could include the leadership issues of determining the leads or calming parents who thought their child should be the "star." The management issues could include handling the funds or putting together a rehearsal schedule. Preparation is the key. The interviewer asks about leadership and management, and the candidate must have outstanding examples with specific details.

Organizational Fit

All the personal and professional characteristics are aimed at addressing the question, "Assuming the candidate has the necessary talent and skill to do the job, will he fit comfortably within the organizational setting and as a result be able to produce at high levels?" However, to understand the total fit issue, the hiring interviewer needs to have a very good understanding of the organization itself and its culture. Two people with many common factors can be entirely different in terms of their fit. "Fit" in an organization tends to be something that is too often neglected until there is a problem. Then there is great concern with it.

CAREER PROFILE
Lack of Fit

The consumer products company with the excellent reputation was in trouble for the first time. After wrestling with the options, the board of directors, on the advice of the CEO, hired a professional manager from the outside to be the president of the company. The new president, with a reputation as a hard driving manager with a consumer products background, knew how to turn a company around.

His style was individualistic and dictatorial. He had been through turnarounds before and he knew what to do. He didn't need input. The results spoke for themselves: higher sales and profits, and a five-year plan in place. In 24 months he had accomplished every financial objective targeted for him.

Yet, internally there was turmoil. For years the organization had developed a decision making style that encouraged staff involvement and team building. Although there was respect for what the president had done, there was no rapport between the president and his direct reports or with anyone else in the organization.

Within 30 months the president was dismissed. The publicly stated reason, his weakness in developing a succession plan, had nothing to do with the reality. His leadership and management philosophy was so jarring to the company's customary procedure that it ultimately created an organizational chasm that even off-the-charts production figures couldn't bridge.   ❑

In this case, the issue hinged on professional characteristics and the president's philosophy of managing an organization and the people in it. Personal characteristics are equally important in achieving success within an organization.

From year to year TV sitcoms change characters dramatically, or they don't return for the new season due to a conflict between the producer and one of the stars of the show. Even if the stars clearly have the right professional credentials (usually the ability to make an audience laugh), their personality and style may make life difficult for those around them.

If the star's ego and demands grow at the same rate as the show's success and popularity, then the working conditions for the cast and crew can deteriorate just as rapidly until there is complete chaos. Finally, decision time comes when the producer fires the star in the interest of the show.

Close

The close is an important part of the interview. The interviewer signals the end of the interview once she has attained all the needed information. She normally tells you that it has been an enjoyable and productive meeting. Human nature is such that, if the interview has been terrific in the interviewer's mind, you have a much greater chance of receiving additional information about the interview process, when the next round of interviews will be held, and when the final decision will be made. In addition, any last questions that you may have are likely to be answered.

The coordinator of the interview team has the responsibility of polling the team to get a consensus concerning each of the candidates. This consensus determines whether a candidate continues in the process or is eliminated from further consideration.

Summary

Interviewers need to have a clear concept of the job specification. They then need to learn about candidates' personal and professional characteristics to make a fair, objective assessment of their potential for success in the organization.

Personal characteristics are defined as:

- Interpersonal skills.
- Style.
- Attitudes and values.
- Motivation.
- Outside interests.

Professional characteristics are defined as:

- Intelligence/technical skills.
- Experience.
- Communication.
- Leadership/management abilities.
- Organizational fit.

STEP 5

Understand
Your Agenda

Why focus on the interview from the candidate's point of view? This is, after all, the real world, and in the real world the interviewer is in control and directs the meeting like a maestro. Candidates therefore need to demonstrate their capabilities by being quick and flexible and having good answers to questions.

This comment came from a senior level manager who was reentering the job market. Her point of view is outdated. In today's job market it is not good enough to be merely qualified. Companies are looking for self-starters who can take the ball and run with it. Since a relationship with a company begins with the first interview, it behooves candidates to be proactive and involved throughout the interview. Granted, the interviewer leads more than the candidate, but the responsibility for a successful interview rests with the candidate just as much as with the interviewer.

This chapter offers new ways for a candidate to approach an upcoming job interview. We encourage our clients to assume the role of:

- Active partners in the discussion.
- Business consultants establishing needs and indicating how they can help to solve them.
- Or salespersons looking to close a deal.

If this seems unattainable, it is only because the approach is new. To act as a business consultant, you must discover the needs of the "customer" (the interviewer) before selling your competencies to help the organiza-

---

INTERVIEW TIP—POSITIVE ATTITUDE

Interviewers look for positive, can-do candidates who are self-starters and eager to accept a challenge.

---

tion solve its problems. An easy way to think of this is "needs sell." The importance of building rapport cannot be overstated in this approach because if the customer isn't comfortable, then the "real" problems may not be revealed. You will discover the interviewer's needs by asking appropriate questions that draw out the issues. The more the "customer" talks and you listen, the better. "Customers" may absolutely know what they need, have no idea, or be somewhere between these two extremes. Once the needs are defined, you "sell" the products (your skills and abilities) that can solve the "customer's" needs or problems.

In this role you are acting as a consultant who both sells and delivers the service. Present your skills and abilities in the best possible light, or you will not make the sale. Likewise, it is also important not to oversell what you can do because you will need to show you can produce. Give an honest answer relative to your abilities, along with examples of your most successful accomplishments, such as:

- The best system you created.
- The largest contribution you made to the bottom line.
- The greatest sale you completed.

If you are a recent graduate, the theory still applies. Use lifetime or school accomplishments as examples.

As a consultant conducting a successful interview, you will need to accomplish a number of objectives. They are:

- Building rapport.
- Questioning (gathering information).
- Developing/clarifying needs.
- Presenting skills and abilities.
- Testing the strength of your candidacy.
- Overcoming concerns.
- Closing.

Prior to examining these steps, let's look at the preparations you need to make *before* the interview.

INTERVIEW TIP—PHYSICAL EXERCISE

Exercising on the day of the interview enables you to relax and gives you a chance to focus. Exercise 75 to 100 percent of a normal workout.

Before the Interview

To be an effective needs-oriented "salesperson," you need to obtain sufficient background information about the company and its people to allow you to conduct a meaningful business discussion by asking the most intelligent questions. Your additional tasks before the interview are (1) a review of your strongest skills and abilities and (2) physical exercise on the day of the interview. Finally, your dress should be professional and on the conservative side, yet appropriate for the industry and company.

During the Interview

In the last chapter we spoke of the importance of interpersonal skills from the moment you meet or speak with someone in the organization. Often you are so focused on the interview itself that you lose sight of what happens from the moment you arrive on site until you leave. Obviously, the way you conduct yourself in these situations should be an extension of your interview behavior.

Building Rapport

Establishing rapport with the interviewer is critical for the candidate. During the first moments of the interview, initial impressions are established. As much as interviewers are trained not to make snap judgments, suspending an opinion is difficult. How you dress, your physical appearance, the way you greet them, whether you smile and make eye contact, the firmness of your handshake, and your walk all meld into that initial composite.

INTERVIEW TIP—PROFESSIONALISM

Be sure you have all pertinent materials and information, such as extra resumes, research reports, annual reports, and financials. Anticipate having to wait before you are interviewed.

Once in the office, you and the interviewer need to spend time getting to know one another. This also gives you a chance to become accustomed to the new environment. Candidates who are geared to the content part of the interview comment that this part of the interview is difficult because they want to get right to the "meat" of the interview. You must remind yourself that rapport building is critical. Forget content for now. If you establish a bond, then content becomes important. If you don't, you are mentally eliminated before you ever mention your skills. The chances are that everyone who has been invited for an interview has the skills to do the job and is probably at about the same level. But are they all alike in terms of personal characteristics, attitudes, values, and management style?

We are sure that they are not. Most of the outstanding interviewers we have met say that, if they meet one candidate who is a pleasant person and is head and shoulders above the rest of the candidates in terms of skills and abilities, it is no contest. They hire that individual. They are also quick to point out that in most instances it doesn't happen like that. With candidates in the same general range, it comes down to the personal factors. And they will all tell you that "fit" is more important than skills at that point. The best technical candidate is often not the one to whom the offer is extended, because another candidate is deemed a better fit in the organization.

The key to effectiveness in this stage of the interview is to take your cues from the interviewer. If the interviewer seems to be relaxed, open, and comfortable with meeting someone new, then your job is easier. You become comfortable fairly fast, and you probably volunteer information about your past and present interests and activities. It becomes easy to keep an interesting and stimulating conversation going even if you don't feel that you are naturally outgoing.

If, however, the interviewer is neither comfortable with himself nor the interviewing process, then your job is much tougher, but certainly not impossible. It may fall to you to keep the conversation going. Whether or not you have reached a comfort level is irrelevant because this is your one, and perhaps only, shot to meet with the interviewer.

This is not as difficult as it sounds. Starting with a smile is tremendously disarming. Be prepared to converse in such a way that you are willing to give a little more detail to your answers. Volunteer some personal information such as where you grew up, your family background, or personal interests and activities. If you help the interviewer to accomplish his task easily and effectively, you'll reap rewards.

INTERVIEW TIP—INITIAL GREETING
A warm smile and a firm handshake make a strong first impression.

CAREER PROFILE
Interpersonal Skills

Rebecca instinctively did the right thing. She had always been able to determine the most uncomfortable person in the room. Her friends could not believe her ability to involve that person in conversation and help him feel comfortable. By the time she left the room, Rebecca had learned intimate details about the person that even close personal friends never knew.

When her children reached high school, Rebecca decided to reenter the work force. She was concerned about her marketability due to her 15-year absence, but she had not taken into account the tremendous interpersonal skills that she had gained through her life experiences. She interviewed with three organizations and, before long, received two job offers.

Once in the position she chose, Rebecca was called into her new boss's office. Carol told Rebecca that the interviewing team had been impressed with her interpersonal skills; in fact, they told Carol they had never met anyone with such strong skills. Carol was curious; she wanted to know where Rebecca had learned such powerful techniques. Rebecca thanked Carol and then laughed. "I haven't had any formal training. In all the volunteer work I've done, and as the mother of two teenagers, I've learned to be both a good listener and persuasive. I've discovered that if you ask a few open-ended questions and genuinely care about what the person has to say, almost everyone will open up."

Is it any wonder that Rebecca was hired?   ❏

If you can learn something about the interviewer's background prior to the interview, it can be a huge help. Clint never interviews without doing all the homework possible on personal background. Somewhere in the history Clint is almost always able to find some common educational bond, mutual friends, and/or interest. This information often helps Clint to cut through numerous layers of surface rapport to reach a deeper personal level. When discussing mutual friends, the interviewer is able to reach a faster comfort level through association. The thought process is, "If Clint is Peter's friend [someone the interviewer knows], then he must be okay." If Peter also happens to be bright, successful, hard-working, and easy to get along with, then so much the better.

In terms of fit, this may translate to, "Peter is our kind of guy. So you may be our kind of person as well." You can see that, even at this early stage of the interview, fit is becoming important. And, as we have discussed, it remains extremely important throughout the interview.

In some situations, however, you are not able to ascertain any information about the interviewer or other key individuals in the organization. This doesn't mean that you will not be successful. It means that you are probably in the same position as the other candidates, and you have to develop rapport from the initial conversation.

In summary, the candidate should go into this segment of an interview with one cardinal rule: *Do not cut the rapport building short.* You cannot control what the interviewer does, but you can control what you do. The key is to follow the interviewer's lead, while keeping in mind your own agenda. This introductory phase of the interview helps to create an easy conversational exchange. How do you know that the other person isn't a scout leader, jogger, coach, or traveler just like you? If the two of you share the same interests, it makes for an interesting dialog rather than a one way monolog. So relax, smile, go with the flow.

Questioning (Gathering Information)

At the conclusion of the rapport building, a transition is needed to move to the business portion of the meeting. As we have indicated, this is done by the interviewer who might say something like, "I've really enjoyed getting to know a little bit about your personal background and interests. Now I'd like to learn something about your professional background," or "I'm interested in hearing about your career and how it has developed."

No matter what the interviewer's method, the message is that a change is being made. The focus changes from personal background to business background, from "get to know you" to interview "content," Just as clearly, rapport building and fit issues do not go away. They continue to be important throughout the interview.

As you prepare to move into questioning, the information that you have gathered about the company and its people becomes crucial. It gives you enough background to conduct a meaningful business discussion. Now you need the interviewer to help put that information into the right context and continue to educate you. The objective is to learn more about the condition of the company, including prospects for short- and long-term growth, the future direction of the company, some definition of how the organization expects the successful candidate to assist in attaining its goals, and the ideal personal and professional skills to fill the role successfully.

The better the rapport you have established, the easier it is to ask the questions you need to ask. The best way to get a positive and enthusiastic response is to help the interviewer see the benefit of them. You might say, for example, "Mr. Jones, I've received some background from reading your annual report. I'd really appreciate some additional information about the organization, your business goals, and the specific position because then I can target my skills and abilities to assist you in achieving your goals." Imagine how clear this sounds to a bottom line business executive who wants to cut straight to the core. The answer is almost certainly, "Sure, how can I help you?"

Incidentally, if you don't like the way that the question is phrased, change it. The style of this question (or any other one) is not as important as the sincerity and enthusiasm you show when asking it. Any question can be asked hundreds of different ways.

Having attained permission to ask the questions, it is important to know where you are trying to go with your questioning. Typically, you lead from the general to the specific:

- Company and its external environment
- Internal environment
- Goals and objectives
- Department
- Specifics of the job

The final level of exploration is the specific skills necessary to do the job. This can be worded in many different ways. You might ask, "Can you describe the ideal candidate?" Or "Will you describe the personal and professional skills in an ideal candidate?" This information may prove invaluable later. Through an initial understanding of how the position fits into the total company puzzle, you gain an understanding of the specific needs in some sort of priority order. (*Note:* This understanding helps to determine which of your skills to present later on.)

The most important skill in seeking information is the ability to listen. Within the context of the business discussion, you must be able to hear everything that is said without making value judgments.

Developing/Clarifying Needs and Presenting Skills and Abilities

As your questions begin to generate information, you discover seeds of the organization's needs or even a clearer definition of them. This process is called *needs development*. Patience is a virtue at this point. Needs can be misinterpreted if you jump to conclusions. The way the company has tried to deal with a problem is as important as the problem itself. Ask how the proposed solutions have turned out. Understand where there have been successes and failures. Ask why.

It is also important to understand the subtleties of the problem. Do the key managers all see the problem in the same way? If they don't, try to understand why not because it is possible they may have different objectives for the individual to be hired. This can be a politically awkward situation. It can also be a real opportunity for a well-prepared job seeker, since a focus on the issues can help an organization clarify its thinking and obtain management consensus prior to hiring a candidate.

Needs clarifying occurs when you think you understand one or more needs. This may seem redundant but it's not. Perception is a funny thing. You are quite sure that you have heard what has been said, but you need a final test to be sure. You might say, "In light of our discussion, is it fair to say that the three critical objectives for the first few years are 1 ... 2 ... 3 ...?" Or "If I heard correctly, sales forecasting and assuming the responsibility for reaching the objectives are important. Is that correct?" If the response is that you are correct, then you have the information you need.

Let's take an example and see how the interaction might flow. Suppose you have some experience in sales and are interviewing for a sales management position for a high-end, sophisticated product in the health care industry. The interviewer seems to be vague about needs, but at one point says, "We have been too passive. We need a take-charge type of person as we move forward." You have now been given a seed of information that should be developed. Why is the interviewer raising this issue? Is the interviewer concerned about the sales forecast? Was the prior manager weak in the fundamentals of the function? Is there concern about the management of people or resources? Is it a management style issue?

In moving the conversation forward, you might ask, "Could you be a little more specific about taking charge?" Suppose the response was, "Certainly, managing the numbers is one concern." Now there is more than a seed; there is real substance. The conversation might move forward as follows:

> CANDIDATE: Is the concern sales forecasting or ownership of the numbers?
>
> INTERVIEWER: The real concern is ownership of the numbers.
>
> CANDIDATE: Has that been a problem?
>
> INTERVIEWER: The previous two sales managers have forecast revenue dollars, but then did not produce.
>
> CANDIDATE: Were there extenuating circumstances?
>
> INTERVIEWER: No.
>
> CANDIDATE: Unrealistic forecasting?
>
> INTERVIEWER: That, we feel, was part of the problem. The situation was compounded by the lack of willingness to accept responsibility for the forecast. The sales manager always had an excuse if the numbers were not met.

As a need is identified, you may have a strong desire to jump in with the various ways that you can help the company to solve the problem. Resist the urge. This is most difficult in areas where you have previously accomplished what is being sought. You must first be sure that you understand the need as it exists in this company. Ask additional questions to further define the need. Sometimes there are major differences between your first impression and the actual need, and sometimes subtle but important refinements have to be made in your first impressions. Suppose, for example, the candidate continued, "Can you tell me the process by which the revenue forecasts are determined?"

The answer to this question may further clarify the situation. Is senior management being unreasonable and perhaps autocratic in the establishment of the revenue forecast, or has a reasonable process been employed? Once the need has been defined and clarified, the interviewer normally expects you to respond with how you would react in the situation. Although this is jumping ahead to product presentation (how your skills and abilities can help to solve the problem), it is the natural flow to the conversation. Consequently, there are usually a series of leaps back and forth from need definition and clarification to product presentation and then back again to develop another need.

In theory, there is some question as to whether this is a better progression for the candidate—or would it be wiser to draw out all the needs and then indicate how your skills could help to solve the organization's problems? In reality, however, it usually doesn't matter. Most interviewers simply don't have the patience to wait until all the needs are developed. They become irritated and that affects you negatively. The interviewer needs to complete his agenda in a timely manner by moving from topic to topic, completing a discussion, and then moving on to a new issue.

Let's assume that the sales forecasting has been done in a reasonable manner and that market conditions appear to be acceptable. As you mentally prepare to respond to the need, you draw on the experiences that give evidence of your abilities to perform successfully and provide proof of your abilities by offering verifiable examples of your successes. If you do not have experience in the area, the alternative is to tell the interviewer how your skills and abilities have prepared you to perform successfully. Let's see how the example might continue.

INTERVIEW TIP—DEVELOPING NEEDS

Ask what the interviewer's problems are and confirm that you understand them before you tell him how you can help to solve them.

CANDIDATE: The process you've described in arriving at the sales forecasting sounds reasonable to me. That's approximately the method I use to forecast. We also had a second set of numbers that were our "stretch objectives" as a challenge to shoot for. But we were evaluated based on reaching our primary objectives.

INTERVIEWER: What responsibility did you bear for reaching those objectives?

CANDIDATE: Prior to being hired, I was told they were mine. I owned them. If I made them I was successful. If I didn't, I failed for that cycle. The organization felt so strongly because my numbers were fed into the CEO's earning forecast and his success was dependent on my success. The balance was to create a set of numbers that were a challenge yet realistic in relation to industry and market conditions. Needless to say, I had input from others on the management team.

INTERVIEWER: How successful were you?

CANDIDATE: I'm proud to say we hit our numbers in seven out of eight years. And there were clear reasons, beyond our control, that caused the one loss.

INTERVIEWER: That's impressive. Were the numbers enough of a challenge?

CANDIDATE: The business grew 15 percent per year over that period of time. In addition, we hit our "stretch objectives" four out of the eight years.

During the discussion the interviewer gives verbal signals concerning his interest in pursuing this line of questioning. Suppose, for the sake of our case study, that you want the conversation to move to a discussion of the sales force.

CANDIDATE: Are there any areas where you have had concerns or faced specific frustrations with the sales force?

INTERVIEWER: We have experienced frustration in a number of areas.

CANDIDATE: Have you been able to identify one or two key concerns?

INTERVIEWER: Our track record is extremely inconsistent in hiring quality staff.

Another need may have been identified. It takes some more development and clarifying to be sure.

CANDIDATE: Are you able to offer a competitive salary and benefit package?

INTERVIEWER: Yes. That's not an issue.

CANDIDATE: Is there consistency in your recruiting and hiring guidelines?

INTERVIEWER: Can you give me a "for instance"?

CANDIDATE: Have you come to grips with the technical ability versus selling ability debate?

INTERVIEWER: No, that is an ongoing issue. Some regional managers believe one thing, some believe another. One of our problems is that each manager acts autonomously.

CANDIDATE: How about the characteristics that you look for in a candidate?

INTERVIEWER: Unfortunately, we don't have consistency there either. Can you tell me what you look for in a candidate and how successful you have been with hires you have made?

Okay, now it's the candidate's turn. The interviewer has been patient, has identified a need and has begun to clarify the need. Now there is a strong desire to hear from the job applicant. Any effort to raise other needs by the candidate at this time could easily be seen as an effort to stall because the candidate has no position on the issue or no experience in that area.

CANDIDATE: Certainly. Let me start with the technical ability versus selling ability debate as an overview. If I can find an ideal candidate who has technical ability and sales ability, it's simple. I hire the person. If I don't have the ideal, then my experience has taught me to make my trade-off on the side of the sales ability or potential.

INTERVIEWER: So you would hire the one with the stronger selling skills.

CANDIDATE: Yes. I've had greater success leaning that way.

INTERVIEWER: Good. That's the CEO's experience as well. What characteristics do you look for?

A little good news in an interview doesn't hurt now and then. The CEO agrees with your position!

CANDIDATE: In terms of a sales profile I look for certain general characteristics and certain specific ones. General characteristics would include someone who (1) understands the customer and what it takes to make a sale, (2) is hungry for commissions, (3) has familiarity with the territory, (4) is intelligent and organized, and (5) makes an excellent appearance and communicates well.

INTERVIEWER: Which of these is most important?

CANDIDATE: Hungry for commissions. The drive to sell.

INTERVIEWER: I agree. I will want to talk about that some more. But you said that you look for certain specific criteria as well. Can you tell me about some of those?

CANDIDATE: The very nature of the high-ticket item dictates that the sale has to be approved at a high level in the client organization. The salesperson needs business sophistication equal to the task. Consequently, I look for a number of specifics: (1) an understanding of the various buying groups; (2) a track record selling capital equipment to hospitals

---

INTERVIEW TIP—PROBLEM SOLVING

You must be willing to take some risks in discussing how you might solve a problem, but you don't want to appear inflexible or dogmatic. You might say, "We've tried X and had some success" or "Have you tried Y?"

---

or a lot of sales potential; (3) an ability to converse technically and financially; (4) skills in life cycle costing; and (5) an understanding and ability to sell the technical benefits of new equipment versus present equipment.

INTERVIEWER: Do you place any priority order on these?

CANDIDATE: I think that these fall into the category of must have or must learn. They are all important.

INTERVIEWER: I agree. What kind of a track record have you had with the retention of sales staff?

CANDIDATE: We averaged approximately 10 hires per year over eight years and 60 are still with the company.

The candidate (unless redirected by the interviewer) could continue to pursue this line of questioning, or go back to the issue of how to find a "hungry salesperson," or move to a new topic. The candidate has learned about two needs: a take-charge sales manager and the hiring of staff. In each instance the need has been developed short of exhausting the interviewer's patience, and then the candidate was able to target skills and accomplishments that demonstrated his ability to perform successfully in the areas where the company needed assistance.

Let's follow one more trail from need development to candidate presentation. Suppose the interviewer volunteered that he had a specific interest in the evaluation of the sales force.

INTERVIEWER: Can you tell me how you evaluate a sales force?

CANDIDATE: I'm used to setting quantitative and qualitative objectives with sales personnel. Would you like to discuss both or focus on one area?

INTERVIEWER: I'm more interested in quantitative objectives.

Note: The last question helps to define the interviewer's interest and allows the candidate to remain focused.

CANDIDATE: If I could ask just a few questions about your present procedures, it will help me to focus my answer.

INTERVIEWER: Sure.

CANDIDATE: Do you presently rank sales personnel?

INTERVIEWER: Yes, we do.

CANDIDATE: Are they then compared to a median sales level?

INTERVIEWER: Yes.

CANDIDATE: Is there a weighted average taking account of such things as difficulty of the territory?

INTERVIEWER: No, we haven't given any weighting to those kinds of factors.

CANDIDATE: Is it a matter of time before someone in the lowest 10 percent incurs the wrath of God?

INTERVIEWER: Not necessarily; it depends on the individual regional manager. Some protect their people, some protect their friends, and some don't protect anyone. But tell me, how you would handle the situation?

CANDIDATE: One last question. What remedial process is employed before the low-producing employee is released?

INTERVIEWER: That is hard to say. It really depends solely on the good will of the regional manager.

That's it. The candidate's time is up. It is time to respond—now. Anything less turns the interviewer into an unhappy camper.

CANDIDATE: It's a difficult process to recruit, hire, and train an effective salesperson. Consequently, evaluation decisions should follow policy and be professional and logical. I believe you have to track progress and compare it across the board. I also think the comparison must be based on a weighted score that takes into account the difficulty of the territory and a series of other variables. When an individual is in the lowest 10 percent, I think an analysis should be undertaken to find out why. If there are extenuating circumstances, they should be noted. If there is no apparent reason, I believe there should be a remedial plan.

INTERVIEWER: A remedial plan? Tell me more.

CANDIDATE: The plan should be positive with the intent to assist the employee to improve. While in a remedial situation, there should be monthly monitoring. If, however, even with assistance the same trend continues, then the employee should be notified that his job could be in jeopardy. Any decisions regarding an employee should be made with input from all the managers who interact with that person.

INTERVIEWER: Has that type of program proven effective for you?

CANDIDATE: Yes, it has. Employees like it because it is designed to be helpful and fair for as long as possible, and senior management likes it because the focus is to upgrade staff continually.

INTERVIEWER: But isn't that too long a time to keep a weak performer?

CANDIDATE: The process sounds longer than it really is. It was actually necessary to put approximately 20 people into the remedial procedure. In six of the cases, the procedure was probably unnecessary because it appeared, in hindsight, that the low performance was due to circumstances beyond the control of the salesperson (economic conditions). Of the remaining 14, eight left shortly after they were put in the remedial plan, and four of the remaining six improved and the other two were asked to leave.

INTERVIEWER: That's very interesting. Did the individuals feel the procedure was fair?

CANDIDATE: No one ever likes to hear bad news. But from all we could gather they felt they had been informed and given an honest chance to improve. And, perhaps more important, it seemed to have a positive effect on the remaining sales force.

A third need has now been developed and addressed. Before going much further and making mistaken assumptions, the candidate should clarify that the needs just discussed are the critical needs. Logic would dictate that they should be the key needs, but once in a while the conversation drifts away from the interviewer and secondary needs are discussed first.

CANDIDATE: Is it reasonable for me to assume that hiring a take-charge sales manager, the recruitment and hiring of quality staff, and effective evaluation, especially as it relates to meeting revenue objectives, are critical objectives to the organization?

INTERVIEWER: Yes, that's right.

CANDIDATE: Are there others?

INTERVIEWER: There are, but they're not as important as the three you just mentioned.

This is an important step. Now the candidate has surpassed conjecture, by requesting confirmation and receiving it. This information helps for the remainder of the interview and the thank you letter. The candidate would never have been sure had he not asked.

INTERVIEW TIP—BUSINESS EXAMPLES

Never tell the interviewer how to "fix" his problem. He may have been trying to fix it for some time without success. Rather, say something like, "I've dealt with problems like that. We have had some success trying a ... b ... c...." Discuss accomplishments.

It could also be helpful in future interviews if the next interviewer holds to the same order of critical objectives. But that has to be tested carefully when the next interview comes. Incidentally, this is an excellent way for you to test the organization to see if there is consistency from one manager to another. Consistency usually builds confidence and a sense that the organization is well managed and knows where it is going.

Testing the Strength of Your Candidacy and Overcoming Concerns

As a conversation progresses, the interviewer accumulates additional information about the applicant. The better the preparation and the fit of the candidate, the higher the interviewer's comfort level will be. No matter how successful the candidate is, however, the interviewer has questions or concerns about the candidate's skills and abilities relative to the specific job needs in one or more areas. The concerns may be caused by something that was (or was not) discussed. It may be caused by a word here or a phrase there. There may have been a misunderstanding of a question asked or an answer given or of a nonverbal sign that left a little question.

Frankly, this is natural. Part of this relates to the fact that seldom does a candidate fill the job specification 100 percent. Another part relates to the role of the interviewer in the negatively oriented screening process. The very nature of the process speaks to finding the things that are wrong so that another person can be screened out. The candidate must be prepared to counter that thought process.

A concern in the mind of the interviewer is not fatal. It can often be corrected, sometimes easily, especially if it is a misunderstanding. What can be fatal is a concern that is not corrected by the end of the interview. It then becomes the damning statement we discussed earlier when the interviewer said, "You know I really liked Susan; there was just one thing she said...." The need to deal with concerns, then, should be clear and obvious. Yet the interviewer does not introduce the subject and the vast majority of job seekers won't touch this issue. Why not?

Dealing with concerns or potential weakness in any form is difficult under the best of circumstances. When the concerns deal with your skills, abilities, or personality, it is that much tougher. But we ask you to balance the difficulty of this task with the need to have the information out on the table where you can deal with it and perhaps make it go away. To us it's no contest. Having the information is crucial.

The issue, then, becomes finding the best method to test this area while maintaining your comfort level and that of the interviewer. The best method, perhaps, is to return to a previous discussion and request a comparison between the targeted professional and personal characteristics and your own. You might ask:

"Mr. Jones, earlier I asked you to define the targeted professional and personal characteristics for this position. Now that you know a little more about me, can you compare my characteristics with the targeted ones?"

Or, "Mr. Jones, now that we have had an opportunity to talk about the position, I feel more confident than ever that I can be of assistance to your organization. Do you have any concerns about my abilities to do the job or fit into the organization?"

Having asked the question, the job applicant must now be ready for the response and how to deal with it. The candidate has asked a very direct question that requires an open, direct response. Some interviewers are able to deal with the question openly and some have problems with it. If you hear a vague response like, "Oh, I think your skills are fine" or "You certainly could do the job," you are probably not being given the information you requested. You might come back and say, "I appreciate those kind words. I am feeling good about the fit as well. What I was trying to do was to see if you had any concerns about my ability in any specific area so that I could address them while we're together." This again lays the issue right out there.

At this point there is either a response and a dialog—or not. If you sense that the interviewer is incapable of dealing with the issue directly or is too uncomfortable to deal with it, then you have no choice but to move on. However, take heart, because many interviewers are able to deal with this discussion more openly and honestly than you think. Remember that job seekers don't get these issues out on the table not because of the interviewer, but often because they don't ask.

Let's suppose that the interviewer is willing to deal with your question. The response to your question can be varied. At the positive end the interviewer may say, "I'm feeling very good about your background and abilities. I am comfortable with what I've heard." You may want to come back to ask about concerns in specific areas or, if your intuition tells you the comments were genuine, you may accept them at face value. A response totally at the negative end is highly unlikely since the organization has spent time and money attempting to screen out individuals who do not have the technical skills before they reached the interview process.

What you are most likely to hear is something in the middle that gives positive feedback yet raises a legitimate concern. Let's go back to the example of the candidate seeking the sales management position. In response to the question about the ability to do the job, the interviewer might respond, "I am very comfortable with your responses to my questions. My concern lies in your ability to manage and grow a large sales force. Your largest previous experience is with a sales force of 200 people, isn't it?"

Okay, a concern has been raised. Now your preparation gets the real test. The question in front of you demands a response, and you don't have a lot of time to prepare your response. Yet, obviously, this needs to be your best prepared and presented response. One that you would spend a weekend on if you had the time, but the reality is that you only have a few seconds to gather your thoughts. However, you've spent the time prior to the interview identifying strengths and weaknesses and preparing answers to potential weaknesses. You're ready. You say:

> Mr. Jones, I did say that I had responsibility for 200 people as a regional sales manager. What we haven't had an opportunity to discuss is the experience I had replacing Sonya Hopkins when she was out for one year with her heart condition. I was selected from among ten regional managers to replace her while she was ill. For the first few months I was merely "holding the fort," but once it became apparent that Sonya was going to be out a long time, my role changed. I was given full resources and assumed all of her functions and responsibilities, including supervising a 500 person sales staff.

The conversation might continue as follows:

INTERVIEWER: That's interesting. What happened when Sonya returned to work?

CANDIDATE: I was asked to assume responsibility for the largest, most profitable yet troubled territory in the region.

INTERVIEWER: What territory did the company assign you?

CANDIDATE: The New York area. The office had been off its numbers for five straight years, had terrible morale problems and a huge turnover. I can honestly say that in the two years I have been in the New York metropolitan region, I learned a great deal and have had almost every problem imaginable.

INTERVIEWER: Give me a "for instance."

CANDIDATE: I had a salesman who was a 25-year employee and had been one of the company's most effective salespeople until his wife became gravely ill and died. He then began to drink, and his productivity level slipped to an unacceptable level.

INTERVIEWER: Were you able to help him?

CANDIDATE: I believe so. He was a valued employee whom the company wanted to save. We certainly had our ups and downs while we were

---

INTERVIEW TIP—EYE CONTACT

Make eye contact throughout the interview. This is particularly critical when being asked about potential concerns or weaknesses.

---

trying to correct the problem, but we had a remedial plan in place and needed to implement it.

INTERVIEWER: How did it end up?

CANDIDATE: His life started to get back on track, and he eventually reached a solid productivity. He did not reach his former level but was three times higher than when he was having problems.

The conversation should continue for as long as the interviewer finds that it is productive and until all of the concerns are raised and addressed.

Does this exchange guarantee that the interviewer's concerns are overcome? Absolutely not. But it defines the concerns, gets them out in the open, and gives you the best shot at resolving them. In the example, you not only had a chance to resolve the interviewer's concerns, but also had an opportunity to reinforce a number of your skills and abilities. You may also have the opportunity to present additional skills that afford the opportunity to continue the business dialog. This extends the time you are with the interviewer, which increases the probability of success.

Closing

It is the interviewer's responsibility to close the meeting. What many job seekers forget or are reluctant to do, however, is to determine what happens next regarding their candidacy. Rather, there is a tendency to sit passively and wait until the company initiates contact. By employing the passive strategy, the candidate loses the opportunity to understand what is happening.

Suppose, for example, you receive a job offer from another company with a defined time frame to let the organization know whether you accept. And suppose that this most recent interview is with the company in which you have the greatest interest. You see, it suddenly becomes critical for you to know when a decision will be made. Let's go back and follow our sample interview through to a possible conclusion.

INTERVIEWER: I've enjoyed meeting you and getting to learn about your background. I think I have all of the information I need. I'd like to thank you for coming in.

CANDIDATE: I've enjoyed the time as well. I feel that you are doing some really exciting things and I'd love to help you move forward with your objectives. Can you tell me how the process will move from here?

INTERVIEWER: Let's see. I believe that I'm the fourth person you've met. Is that correct?

CANDIDATE: Yes, that's right.

INTERVIEWER: There will be one more round of two or three interviews with the executive vice-presidents and president.

CANDIDATE: Can you tell me whether I'll be recommended for that round of interviews?

INTERVIEWER: You are the last person I'm interviewing and I'm impressed. You will be moving to the next round.

CANDIDATE: Thank you. I'm excited about that. Can you tell me how many other candidates will be moving to the final round and when those interviews will occur?

INTERVIEWER: There are two other candidates, and we are going to try to schedule them for next week.

CANDIDATE: Will the final decision be made soon?

INTERVIEWER: Probably within three weeks.

CANDIDATE: Is there any additional information that I should have to prepare for the interviews?

INTERVIEWER: I don't think so. Frankly, I'm surprised that you have been able to obtain as much information as you have about the organization. That's impressive.

CANDIDATE: You were extremely helpful in my preparation and I wanted you to know how much I appreciate your help.

INTERVIEWER: You're welcome. You'll hear from me toward the end of next week. Can you find your way out?

CANDIDATE: Yes. Thanks for your time.

INTERVIEWER: Good-bye.

Do you know everything there is to know going forward? No, but you have learned some important information. You are going to the final round of interviews with two other candidates in about a week. The final decision should be made in about three weeks. Furthermore, your efforts at preparation regarding the company and its people seem to have been successful. This is all excellent feedback and indicates that you have handled yourself in a professional manner. You are also managing your job campaign because you know when and under what conditions the decision will be made.

A final point: By reaching the finals, you have successfully handled all aspects of the interviewing process that are within your control. From this

---

INTERVIEW TIP—TIMETABLE

Ask about the interviewer's timetable for filling the position. Knowing that enables you to manage the timing of your job campaign effectively.

---

point, personal chemistry and the interviewer's definition of fit are the determining factors unless one of the candidates "shoots himself in the foot." These things are out of your control. Your goal in the final round is to relax, be yourself, and interview the same way you have previously. If you receive the offer, great. If you don't, then move forward confidently. Your interviewing technique is effective. The same personal and professional characteristics demonstrated in the next interview may well help you to secure the offer.

After the Interview— the Thank You Letter

A thank you letter to each interviewer should be considered an extension of the interview—and an absolute necessity. Few job applicants do this and it really makes a difference. The thank you letter is usually a few paragraphs in length with each paragraph covering a different topic. The letter should not be more than one side of a page. The initial sentence should refer to something specific from your conversation so that it becomes a personal, rather than a business letter. You might say: "I enjoyed meeting you and learning about your objectives ..." or "Thank you for meeting with me and sharing your thoughts on the direction of the company." Then indicate your interest and excitement in the position and the company.

The second paragraph is an opportunity to reinforce those of your beliefs that agree with the company's direction or methodology. It's a way to continue bonding with the interviewer and to indicate that you are in synch with the company. This can include ways that your skills could be helpful going forward.

A third paragraph is optional. This is a chance to mention the skills and abilities that were not discussed during the interview but that you feel will further your candidacy. Sometimes a critical skill or ability was not discussed due to time constraints or due to the direction of the conversation. This is an opportunity to rectify the oversight.

The final paragraph is a review of the next steps and a closing. You might end, for example, with "I look forward to hearing from you in a week to schedule the next interviews."

Occasionally, a candidate is given an assignment to complete as part of the evaluative process. Assignments should be of the highest quality, presented in a professional style, and completed on time.

Summary

The best means of accomplishing the candidate's agenda is by approaching the interview as a sales call. The sales call involves:

- Building rapport.
- Questioning (gathering information).
- Developing/clarifying needs.
- Presenting skills and abilities.
- Testing the strength of your candidacy.
- Overcoming concerns.
- Closing.

Think Win-Win Interaction

In the last two chapters we examined what the interviewer and the candidate would like to accomplish in the interview without regard to the human interaction. Interaction adds the possibility that both agendas cannot be accomplished at the same time. Therefore, there has to be a give and take that allows the interviewer and you to accomplish your objectives within a congenial, interactive atmosphere. Understanding this interaction and how it can help you to be successful are the subjects of this chapter and the next.

Let's see how a conversation might take place in a social setting, and then we can discuss the complexities added to a conversation in an interview setting.

A Social Conversation

Everything was running behind schedule—from the car service that picked me up late, to the flight to San Juan that left 45 minutes late for no apparent reason, to the pilot of the tiny plane from San Juan to St. Thomas who seemed in no hurry to take off anytime in this decade. So I found myself careening down the gangplank to the rickety dock at Red Hook only to see the tiny ferry to St. John chugging off without me. With a choice expletive I slammed my luggage down and kicked it toward a bench.

"It's not that bad," a voice offered. "It only takes ten minutes for the ferry to get to the Caneel Bay dock. It'll be back again in under a half hour."

I looked up to see a guy about my age focusing a camera on the departing ferry.

"You seem to know what you're talking about," I responded.

"I do. This is the fourth year I've come here. You're from New York, aren't you?" he said with a smile.

"Is it that obvious?" I answered.

"Well, you remind me of myself before I got transferred from New York to our Minneapolis office."

"No wonder you're here," I said. "This must be heaven compared to the temperatures you just left in Minnesota."

"12 below and that was at noon. How did you happen to hear about this resort?"

"My cousin escapes here as often as she can," I answered. "She loves the snorkeling."

"She has great taste," he said. "The snorkeling at Trunk Bay is the prettiest in the Caribbean in my opinion."

The conversation continued effortlessly. Chip and I became friends and snorkeled together twice that week. We have stayed in touch since that trip. Our initial conversation had several key components that contributed to its success:

- We established a rapport.
- We both clearly enjoyed the conversation.
- We found some topics that were stimulating and interesting to both of us.
- We both participated actively in the conversation.
- We both talked approximately the same amount.

Complexities in Job Interviewing

In the previous chapters we identified three basic objectives that must be accomplished for you to be successful in an interview:

Objective 1: Recognize the importance of building rapport. If the interviewer "falls in love" with you, then all aspects of the interview are viewed more positively.

Objective 2: Accomplish the interviewer's agenda. The interviewer's agenda is to determine whether your skills, abilities, and personality fit the company's needs and environment.

Objective 3: Accomplish the candidate's agenda. Your agenda is to identify the major goals of the organization and to sell your abilities to accomplish them.

Achieving these three objectives is no small task, but there's more. It's complicated by the personality style and expectations of the interviewer, none of which you can ignore. The interviewer:

- Is in a favored position.
- Controls the interview.
- Is the buyer.

It is important to examine these conventions because they dictate, to some degree, your behavior in the interview. The interviewer clearly is in a favored position because she has something that you want—a job. As a candidate, you must be sure that you assist the interviewer to accomplish her agenda or you have no chance of being successful.

That the interviewer controls the interview is a time-honored convention. In virtually all interview training (and intuitively if there has been no training), the interviewer is taught that, once the rapport building portion of the interview is completed, she should take control of the interview. This allows her to determine whether your professional skills and abilities and personal characteristics are an outstanding fit within the culture of the organization. This is accomplished, in most cases, by the interviewer's asking short, open-ended questions that seek long, complete answers. You must be aware of the control issue and understand that individual interviewers vary in their need for control. In any event, seeking a change in communication from question/answer to interactive dialog is a critical issue that requires sensitivity and finesse.

The interviewer is the buyer (and you, the candidate, are the seller). Interviewing, from its early stages through the selection of the final few candidates, is a negatively oriented, screening out process. It's like a multilayer sieve that refines flour to its finest state. The interviewer doesn't want to spend time selling candidates on the merits of the company if there is no chance that they will make it to the later stages of the interview process. Consequently, the interviewer would rather spend time evaluating the fit issues and determining where candidates stand in the priority ranking of candidates. Candidates must understand this need as critical to the interviewer's agenda and assist the interviewer to accomplish her goal. What is important to candidates is to do well enough in the interview to have the interviewer's "buy" become a "sell" as she decides that you will proceed in the interviewing process or be offered a position.

Communications Flow

The key to your success in the interview is to become a partner with the interviewer in managing the communications flow, that is, the percentage of talk by each participant. This task is complicated by the conventions we just discussed, including the interviewer's need to remain in control. Yet a change from question/answer to an open, interactive dialog is well worth the effort because it makes the interview more exciting, stimulating, and challenging, and it dramatically increases your chances for success.

The best example we can give to illustrate the point is one that all of us have experienced. Think back to your high school years and identify your two or three best teachers (using any criteria you want). Let's call all the other teachers in your high school the control group. Now let's focus on just one variable, the percentage of talk. Part one is to decide whether the best teachers, on average, talked more or less in their classes than the control group teachers. Part two is to determine what percentage of time each group of teachers talked. When you have your answer, read on.

We'll bet your answer is that the best teachers talked less. Did you guess that the best teachers talked about 50 percent of the time, while the control group teachers talked 80 percent or more of the time? You were right.

Your outstanding teachers probably managed to have stimulating, challenging classes that seemed to fly by because they involved you in interesting material and maintained a highly interactive conversation. Do you see the kind of climate we are trying to create in the interview?

Interview Framework

A simple framework can help us visualize communication flow during various phases of the interview. If we plot the pattern that most interviewers follow, then examine the pattern we would like to see, we'll be able to observe the similarities and disparities. When the agendas are the same, we won't have to worry about conversation management. When there are disparities, we'll recognize what is happening and look for opportunities to improve our position.

The pattern most interviewers want to follow (for a detailed discussion, see Step 4) starts with an interactive rapport building with each participant talking about 50 percent of the time. When the interviewer makes the transition to the business portion, she likes to ask short, open-ended questions and have you talk 85 to 90 percent of the time. She is clearly a buyer at this time. If your answers satisfy her and hit the mark, she allows a

---

INTERVIEW TIP—ANSWERING QUESTIONS

Answer the interviewer's questions directly and concisely. This gives the interviewer confidence that you are willing to help accomplish the agenda.

---

gradual change to 50 percent talk each in the last third of the business portion of the interview. Assuming you are a viable candidate, she does some selling during this time.

Figure 6–1 graphs the communication flow as the interview progresses from phase 1 (on the left), which is the rapport building phase, through phase 5 (on the right), which is the close. The communications flow, which identifies the percentages of candidate and interviewer talk, is shown by line A.

The pattern you as the candidate want to follow (for a detailed discussion, see Step 5) starts with the same interactive rapport building (50 percent talk each) as the interviewer pattern. The difference comes in the business portion, where you would like to continue the same pattern throughout the interview. This provides you with the opportunity to identify the company's needs, to clarify them, and to present your skills and abilities to accomplish the needs. Then you could test your candidacy with the interviewer, overcome any concerns, and accomplish additional rapport building while the interviewer is closing the meeting.

Figure 6-2 graphs the communication flow, which is shown by line B. The phases of the interview describe the candidate's agenda.

Figure 6-3 merges the communication flow of the interviewer model (Figure 6-1) and the candidate model (Figure 6-2). The communication flow is shown by line A (the interviewer's model) and line B (the candidate's model). The gray area shows divergence. The interviewer's and candidate's agendas are identified at the bottom of the graph.

It is clear that the agendas are parallel in phases 1, 4, and 5 and divergent in phases 2 and 3. The divergence (gray area) represents an opportunity for the candidate and the interviewer to change the communications flow from a candidate-dominated pattern (talking 85–90 percent of the time) to one that approaches 50 percent talk each.

INTERVIEW TIP—BUSINESS CONVERSATION

The goal is to create an exciting, stimulating 50–50 percent business conversation throughout the interview.

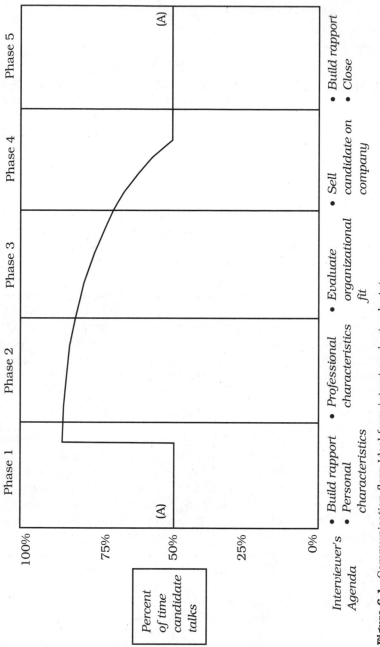

Figure 6-1. Communication flow: Ideal from interviewer's standpoint

Figure 6-2. Communication flow: Ideal from candidate's standpoint

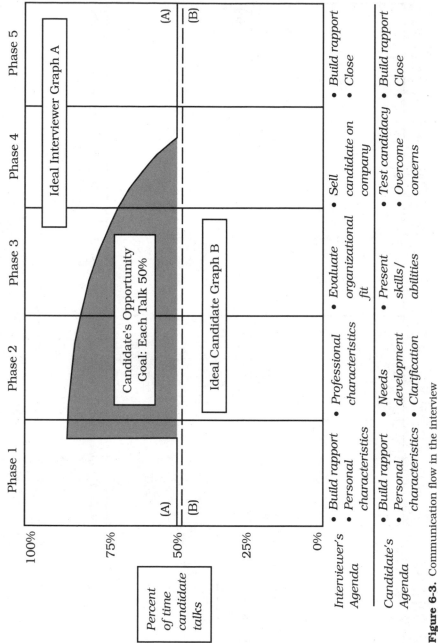

Figure 6-3. Communication flow in the interview

CAREER PROFILE
Business Opportunity

The notion that two participants in a conversation have different agendas certainly isn't new. It happens all the time in social settings. Suppose, for example, you are anticipating meeting Edward, a key business contact. At a reception after a concert someone introduces you to Edward. After the introductions he asks you what you thought of the concert. The focus of the conversation remains on the guest soloists and the excellence of their performance. Soon, the conductor comes by and Edward turns his attention to him. You hide your disappointment. The moment is lost.

Clearly your agenda and Edward's were different. You would have loved for the conversation to turn to business even in that first encounter. Edward's agenda, however, was purely social. Once the disappointment is gone, you realize that it was, in fact, a good encounter because you met Edward and can build on that. You realize it was probably unrealistic to talk business in the first encounter anyway.

But suppose that you're persistent about the relationship. You do some homework about Edward's office supply business and find out that he has increased the business by $50 million in the past four years. It is growing by leaps and bounds, but he is going to need another generation of management if he wants to take the business to the next plateau. You know that your experience working for one of the largest office supply companies is exactly what he needs.

After the next concert you are fortunate to catch him alone. After exchanging pleasantries, you remind him of your first meeting and then say, "I've been reading some wonderful things about your company. You must be excited about your rapid growth." He is genuinely appreciative of your comment and tells you about the business. Edward is amazed to learn how much you know. When he asks what you do, he is extremely interested in both your background and the industry knowledge you could give him. He suggests that you get together for a business lunch to exchange war stories, and you willingly accept. Three months, and a series of meetings later, you happily accept your new job as general manager of Edward's company.   ❏

In these two brief encounters we saw divergent and parallel agendas. Success depended on sizing up the situation and then having the patience to wait for the right moment. When that moment occurred, presentation and content then became important considerations in the successful outcome.

Divergent Phases in the Job Interview

In light of our discussion concerning how much more enjoyable interactive business discussions are for both interviewer and candidate, there should be no issue about changing a boring 85 to 90 percent monolog to an enjoyable encounter. A knowledgeable interviewer must know and want that as well. The change also makes the meeting easier for the interviewer because she doesn't have to take the lead all the time (by asking the next question or changing the direction). Rather the lead can be passed back and forth like actors in a play.

Unfortunately, it's not that simple. While those arguments are true, there's the other side of the coin. The interviewer has been trained to control the conversation and may be more comfortable in that style. The interviewer may also think that it could be viewed as a sign of weakness if she doesn't remain in control.

We've reached the crux of the problem. If the interviewer willingly allows the communications to move away from question and answer toward a business conversation, then she is giving up some authority to dictate communications direction as well as change the communications flow (the percentage of talk by each person). For one interviewer, this is a simple switch that makes a lot of sense. For another, it is a change of style that she might make only as she becomes comfortable with the candidate. For yet another, it is so alien to her personality and comfort level that it is an impossible change.

This poses two major concerns for the candidate. First, he must be able to understand what is happening during the interview and what will probably happen next so that he can respond appropriately. Second, he must be able to read whether the interviewer is willing to allow changes in the communications flow toward an interactive exchange.

Assuming the interviewer is willing and the candidate is able to cause the change to a business discussion (even for a brief period), the percentage of candidate talk in the early part of phase 2 is somewhere between the interviewer's model and the candidate's model. It is closer to 50 percent talk by each participant and dramatically increases the chances for success.

Screening/Hiring Interviewers

We are often asked whether the interview framework is applicable to screening as well as to hiring interviews. The answer is that it applies to both. Some differences between the two types of interviewers are only minor variations on a theme rather than a completely new one.

In the screening process, you are liable to encounter the executive search consultant and then the human resource professional. Their roles are to address professional skills, personal characteristics, and overall fit, as well as to screen out candidates so that the hiring manager has to deal with only a small pool of highly qualified applicants. High on their list are thoroughness, efficiency, and time management. Their preferred styles of interviewing are often to control the meeting by asking open-ended questions having to do with your skills and background and then evaluating your answers (i.e., looking for reasons to eliminate you). If the screening interviewer were only evaluating skills versus a job specification, you might never accomplish any of your agenda. Evaluating personal characteristics and overall fit, however, requires dialog, and dialog affords you opportunities to accomplish your agenda as well. Still, keep in mind that under normal circumstances it will be more difficult for you to move the discussion toward a 50–50 percent business discussion with a screening interviewer than with a hiring interviewer. Your goal is to do the best you can.

The hiring interviewer is usually a line manager who is concerned with finding someone who can perform successfully in the job and who is an excellent fit with those in the company and department. She may begin the interview in a question/answer manner, but often engages in a dialog to find out about you and your skills. The reason for this is that she has a real business need to have a partner (or subordinate) to carry out the mission of the organization. She is less concerned with interviewing procedure than with finding the right person to assist her. This willingness to engage in a business dialog makes it much easier for you to accomplish your agenda. It also creates a more stimulating environment for both you and the interviewer.

Summary

The key components in creating a win-win approach to winning your ideal job are:

- *Build rapport with the interviewer (the "falling in love" process).* If the interviewer "falls in love" with the candidate, all aspects of the interview are viewed more positively and the chances of being hired dramatically increase.

- *Establish an interactive, stimulating (50 percent talk each) conversation.* An interview is the most exciting, stimulating, and fun when it remains interactive from start to finish. The closer you get to 50–50 percent talk throughout all phases of the interview, the better both interviewer and candidate feel about the interview.

- *Assist the interviewer to evaluate your fit in the company.* The interviewer is in a more favorable position (she has the job). It is to the candidate's advantage to assist the interviewer in accomplishing her agenda, which is to decide whether the candidate's skills, abilities, and personality are a good fit in the company's environment.

- *Convert the interviewer's mindset from "buy" to "sell."* As the candidate assists the interviewer to understand his skills, abilities, and personal characteristics, the interviewer becomes more and more comfortable with him. Eventually, the "buyer" (the interviewer as buyer) becomes a "seller" (the interviewer selling the merits of the company to the candidate).

- *Learn the organization's goals and sell your abilities to reach them.* The interviewer begins to assist the candidate to accomplish his agenda once her own is in progress. The candidate's agenda is to draw out the major goals of the organization and to sell his abilities to accomplish those goals.

Create Effective Interview Strategy

The interview framework showed where agendas were parallel and divergent. This chapter gives candidates ideas for interaction in each of those situations.

We will follow the sequence established in the framework, moving from phase 1 to phase 5 of the interview. These headings follow the basic pattern of an interview, that is, as the candidate, you should spend time getting to know someone prior to generating needs, prior to presenting your abilities, prior to closing the interview. However, remember that, in the dynamics of the actual interview, there is a good deal of jumping back and forth from one phase to another.

In phases of the interview where your agenda and the interviewer's are in synch, you can relax and "go with the flow" (phases 1, 4, and 5). In phases where your agendas differ, a little tinkering with interview strategy increases the chances for creating an interactive business conversation and brings better results (phases 2 and 3).

Phase 1: Building Rapport

Interviewer's Agenda:

- Build rapport
- Personal characteristics

INTERVIEW TIP—RELAX

We're serious. Relax! Approach the interview as an enjoyable opportunity.

Candidate's Agenda:

- Build rapport
- Personal characteristics

Note: These headings correspond to the interviewer's agenda and to the candidate's agenda found in Figure 6-3 in the previous chapter.

The interviewer's and candidate's objectives are more similar in the initial phase than in any other phase of the interview. In most cases the interviewer is more than happy to engage in an interactive conversation and is interested in learning about your personal characteristics, building rapport, and conducting the normalcy test discussed earlier. Your agenda is learning about the interviewer's personal characteristics and building rapport. An interactive conversation should be fine with the candidate because it affords an excellent opportunity for you to relax and become comfortable in the new surroundings.

There is usually some small talk, as would happen if you met someone at a party. You might be asked, for example, if you had any trouble with the travel directions. (This is one time in the interview that you might tell an untruth. Even if the directions took you from Chicago to Dallas via Miami, you say, "Oh, the directions were great." Remember that the interviewer or someone close to him gave you the best directions they could.)

Rapport building is a time of great opportunity (and risk) for the candidate. In today's marketplace the best jobs draw a number of highly qualified candidates. The difference between them often comes down to personal chemistry—not technical skills. The interviewer is trying to answer questions like, "Who is the best fit in my organization?" and "Who am I most comfortable with?" Building great chemistry starts at the beginning of the interview.

INTERVIEW TIP—BOND

If the interviewer "falls in love" with you, great things can happen. You may be hired, for example. If rapport is not built, nothing good can happen.

CAREER PROFILE
Rapport Building

A greater percentage of jobs are won (and lost) in phase 1 than you might think. Colin had acquired a strong finance background working for a major oil company. When the company moved out of town he decided to stay behind, since he and his wife had elderly parents living nearby. He searched for a position and identified a company that seemed exciting. When he went to interview with the president for the chief financial officer position, he was somewhat apprehensive. During the rapport building, the president asked Colin about his outside interests. Colin said that he had been handling the financial responsibilities for an addition on his church. The president was surprised and told Colin he was doing the same thing. The one-hour interview lasted two and one-half hours, and Colin was absolutely clear why he won the job.

Kieran had a somewhat similar experience. She held a marketing position for a midwestern defense manufacturer that was bought by another company. Kieran and her husband had no children, but as part of their volunteering they were officials at Special Olympic events for handicapped youngsters. In a short time Kieran landed an interview at her "dream" company in a city in western Michigan. She felt that the interviews went well with her potential boss and his boss. Then Kieran received an added bonus. The vice-president of marketing returned early from a meeting and took the time to meet Kieran. A simple question brought out Kieran's interest in handicapped children. The vice-president, a caring and involved father, had a handicapped child. Kieran did not have to guess why she won the job; her boss told her when he made her the offer.   ❏

In summary, the one thing you don't want to do during this time is to cut off the personal interaction. It almost seems like something that doesn't need to be said but it does. A bright, aggressive person sometimes wants to get down to business. If the interviewer makes small talk for too long, the candidate wants to grab him by the throat and shake him. No matter how

---

INTERVIEW TIP—BUILD RAPPORT

Don't cut rapport building short. The interviewer does it soon enough.

bright and well-qualified they are, these candidates are shortly on the "Don't call me, I'll call you" list. Relax. Enjoy the conversation. See if you can learn something about the interviewer. Let the interviewer begin to "fall in love" with you. Maybe you'll discover some common interests, activities, or people. The chances of being offered a position are significantly higher if the interviewer thinks you're great.

Tactics

- Ask yourself, "Does it look like I am enjoying myself?"
- Smile, laugh (when appropriate).
- Be approachable and friendly.
- Help the interviewer keep the conversation moving.
- Discuss your interests (one may be a mutual interest).
- Identify common experiences and/or friends.
- Show enthusiasm for the interviewer's interests.
- Do not cut off rapport building.
- *Be positive.*

Phase 2: What's Your Background for This Job?

Interviewer's Agenda:

- Professional characteristics

Candidate's Agenda:

- Needs development
- Clarification

Eventually, the interviewer makes the transition to the business portion of the meeting. When this happens, he wants to continue to gather information about your personal characteristics and to learn about your professional background, including general intelligence, technical skills, and experience. This check is to be sure you meet the job specifications. Research concerning your background took place prior to the interview, but face-to-face discussion is also critical. The interviewer wants to trace your career path to be sure it is moving in a steadily upward direction (lateral moves are also acceptable, but be prepared to explain them). He wants to understand why you left each position to gain clues to what drives and motivates you. Although your agenda calls for you to learn about the company, the position, and the people, hold off for a while. Follow the lead of the interviewer.

The style that the interviewer selects is less important than your ability to recognize and react to what is happening. With this recognition, you are in a position to implement strategies that lend themselves to a win-win interview. Let's take the worst case scenario and assume the interviewer directs a question/answer format.

Perhaps the interviewer asks you three, four, or five open-ended questions about your background that require fairly long responses. Suppose the first question is, "Tell me about yourself," or "Why don't you tell me something about your education and career history?" If left unchecked, this pattern quickly adds up to 80 percent candidate talk with little interaction or information gained. An additional concern is that, with all the talk, you must maintain the interviewer's interest.

The best way to stay on track and to keep interviewer interest high is to keep your answers short. This also helps to keep your percentage of talk from skyrocketing. (*Note:* Earlier we discussed the sales research indicating the importance of keeping your answer to 60 seconds.) Then, if the interviewer wants, you can go back and give greater detail on any part of your answer. In response to the question, "Tell me about yourself," the answer might be given as follows:

CANDIDATE: Well, I grew up in suburban New Jersey, about an hour outside of New York. I have one brother who is younger than I am. My father sold industrial heating controls and my mother was a secretary. The love of my life while growing up was sports.

INTERVIEWER: That's interesting.

CANDIDATE: I was recruited to go to Colgate University where I was a political science major and a starter on the basketball team. Along the way I became interested in marketing. After completing my studies at Colgate I enrolled at the Kellogg School at Northwestern. Two years later I completed my MBA.

INTERVIEWER: Then you went to General Foods?

CANDIDATE: Yes, I progressed through the ranks to brand manager of one of our most successful brands. After a period of time I was ready to move to group product manager. Since the organization's timing and mine were out of synch, I interviewed for a position at Quaker Oats and was successful in attaining a position.

INTERVIEWER: Go on.

CANDIDATE: I feel that I have developed a number of skills. I have consistently produced profit for the company, I have been told that I provide charismatic leadership for the organization and that I am a rallying point as we move a company forward. In addition, I feel I have the ability to meld disciplines, such as marketing, research, and manufacturing, to form a cohesive team.

INTERVIEW TIP—LENGTH OF ANSWER

Keep your answers short. No answer should be longer than 60 seconds.

When to Pop *Your* Question

As you answer a number of the interviewer's questions, a comfort level starts to develop. The interviewer gets to a point where he is at ease with the way things are happening in the meeting and with the answers you are giving (due to your outstanding preparation). You won't need anyone to tell you when the interviewer is comfortable with the conversation flow. Your antennae signal you.

As the interviewer's comfort rises, windows of opportunity begin to appear for you to do needs development. In a question and answer format they usually occur at the end of one of your answers. You know when your answer is going to end. The interviewer doesn't. If you end your answer by completing your thoughts on the information requested, then you are asked another question and the pattern continues. But suppose that, instead of merely ending your thought, you ask a question that directly relates to the discussion, one that seeks information about the interviewer's business needs. Let's look at an example.

> INTERVIEWER: Can you tell me about your duties in your current position?"
>
> CANDIDATE: Yes, my duties consist of three major components. They are [elaborate on your duties]. Can you tell me about some of the skills you are looking for?

Frankly, the candidate's question can be worded in any number of ways. For example:

"Are any of my recent responsibilities similar to your needs?"

"Can you tell me something about the position you are filling?"

"Can you tell me about the objectives the successful candidate will have in the first few months?"

If your "read" is correct and the interviewer has reached a comfort level, he answers your question. During the brief time that he is answering the question, you are obviously not talking, which slightly lowers your percentage of talk. However briefly, you have switched to a business discussion or conversation format. When you ask the question, however, there is a range of options available to the interviewer.

The worst thing that can happen is that the interviewer doesn't like the fact that you have asked a question and doesn't respond or indicates he would rather not answer a question at this time. Let's say the interviewer just went right on and asked another question. This is rare, but, if it happens, assume that you made an incorrect read and flip back into your "answer the question" mode. Patience is critical with this interviewer. You then have to read the signals for a period of time before you try again. Even then, you may not feel very comfortable trying to ask a question because you were rejected the first time. Given an opportunity to ask another question, you may be more comfortable if you explain why you need the information: "If you could define the department's key goals over the next year or two, it will help me to target my skills and abilities to those needs."

Another possibility is that the interviewer answers the question and then immediately reverts to the question/answer format. This is clearly moving in a positive direction. The fact that he responded expresses a willingness to give some information although his comfort level remains with the question and answer style. The behavior, however, leaves the door open for you to try again in a few minutes. (*Note:* We are not suggesting that you ask a question after each question you are asked. Use judgment.)

A third possibility is that the interviewer is receptive to the question and provides an opportunity for dialog. Then, after the topic is fully covered in a conversational format, the interviewer switches back to a question/answer mode. This option dramatically changes the percentage of talk (toward 50–50 percent) during the dialog period and gives you an opportunity to raise questions and generate information.

Finally, the dream option is that the interviewer is receptive to your question, provides an opportunity for dialog, and does not switch back to a question/answer format. This causes a total switch to a conversational format, changes the percentage of talk to close to 50 percent each, and provides an opportunity for you to be an equal partner (almost) in the conversation.

If the last two options seem to be a fantasy, they're really not. Remember that a business discussion or conversation is a much more relaxed and comfortable style for the interviewer, and the switch often makes the meeting more interesting and informative. Consequently, there is strong incentive to remain in a business discussion. Once in this mode, if the interviewer continues to feel that he is getting the information he needs, there may not be great incentive to change.

Changing Gears

As you become comfortable with the concept, you find that you can encourage a switch in any number of ways. For example, Rick went back for a second interview with an investment bank. He knew that strategic planning meetings had been taking place during the three weeks since he had visited; his agenda was to learn about the managing director's current thinking and how that would affect his previous discussions. At the conclusion of the personal rapport portion of the interview, Sandra began a question/answer format with Rick. After a few minutes of straight question and answer, Rick said, "You know it has been about three weeks since we last met. I wonder if you could review your current thinking on department direction? It would help to bring me up to speed." The comment was perfect. It fit within the context of the discussion, and asked for help in understanding what was happening. Sandra answered the question and the discussion became an open dialog. The meeting remained a discussion from that time forward. You cannot always completely change a pattern, but you don't know what you can do until you try.   ❏

Seeking Clarification

Another technique for changing the communications flow and testing your focus is to ask for clarification. This works well when the interviewer is reluctant to change from question/answer to business discussion or when you are not sure what information interests the interviewer. Suppose, for example, the interviewer asks, "What are some of your outstanding accomplishments?" This question is so broad that you have no idea what information might be of interest. The more direction you can get, the more you can focus your answer. You might proceed as follows: "Mr. Jones, is there a particular job or area of my background on which you would like me to focus?"

You might hear, "Anything you want to tell me," and in that case you take your best shot at giving your outstanding accomplishments as briefly as possible. Our experience, however, is that this does not happen as often as you might think. In business, executives are busy and many prefer to get to the heart of the matter. Consequently, you might hear, "Certainly, I'm most interested in your new product development experience" or "Tell me about your experiences at Citibank."

Even this brief exchange has helped you in two ways. It has focused the conversation toward the interests of the interviewer, and it has slightly reduced your percentage of talk moving the discussion closer to a business discussion.

As you begin to have success in changing the conversation flow, you're going to be looking for information about the company and people in addition to specific information about the position. Your interest at this point is threefold:

1. You need to gain information about the company's needs before you can sell your skills and abilities.

2. You need to start now, right at the beginning of the first interview, to gather data to decide whether you want to invest a portion of your business career in this kind of company—the due diligence for the "buy."

3. You want to lay the groundwork for what you want to accomplish later in the meeting. For your due diligence study, you have to ascertain how the interviewer sees the position being structured (to whom it reports, authority/resources, accountability), the goals (six months, one year, three years), and how the individual is evaluated (financial and nonfinancial variables). In addition, one of the best questions for future reference is, "Would you describe the ideal candidate for this position?" The answer to this question gives valuable information to assist you when it comes to testing your candidacy.

The Need to Listen and Listen and Listen

To this point we have been talking about what candidates might do to move the conversation slightly toward a business discussion. The purpose of doing that is simple: The earlier in the meeting that you can learn about the needs of the organization and begin to get a sense of what can be done to solve the organization's problems, the more time you have to sell your skills and abilities to solve those needs.

Developing organizational or individual needs requires the ability to listen to the other person's business problems, understand and care about them, and be able to restate them accurately. It requires listening skills, the ability to ask penetrating questions, and then to synthesize the information given. Finally, the ability to show empathy and a legitimate sense of concern are needed. The hardest part of listening for many people is to resist the urge to start thinking about what to say next. You may have an impatient side that wants to jump in and speak before the other person has even finished a sentence or question. You feel that all you need is a thread of an idea. "Hold it, hold it," that impatient side says, "I can finish that thought. I can add value to the conversation." Active listening requires concentration and discipline. It's hard work, but it's an invaluable interview tool.

Questioning and Assessing Needs

After listening (and listening and listening), questioning skills and formulating the needs become important. It normally takes a good deal more
concentrated questioning than one thinks to understand someone else's
needs. After all, you're coming to the discussion cold or with only partial
information, while the interviewer has been living with the needs every
day and understands the problem inside and out. Problem solving skills
can be particularly helpful at this time. Intelligent candidates realize that
the interviewer is their greatest resource. It demonstrates strength and intelligence to ask for help. For example, "Am I correct that your real need is
in changing your sales philosophy and mission and not the constitution of
your sales force?" Once the need is developed, you are able to confirm the
needs, as discussed in the chapter dealing with the candidate's agenda.

In summary, the critical issue in this phase of the interview is that you
have to support the interviewer in establishing his style for the business
portion of the interview and in accomplishing his agenda. You cannot
have a successful interview unless the interviewer does. Once the interviewer gains a comfort level and obtains the information that is important
to him, then, and only then, do windows of opportunity appear for you to
pursue your interests. Your agenda is to determine the needs of the organization and to confirm them. If, during the interaction, it is possible to
change the conversation from question/answer to business discussion,
then the potential is the greatest for a stimulating, enjoyable, and productive conversation for the interviewer and you.

Tactics

- Focus on the interviewer's needs first, and satisfy them.
- Learn the interviewer's preferred style (question/answer, business dis-
  cussion, lecture).
- Anticipate what will happen next in the interview.
- Change the format from question/answer to business discussion. (Your
  objective is to talk 50 percent of the time.)
- Learn about the company, the position, and the people.
- Adhere to the 60-second rule (no answer longer than 60 seconds).
- If you're not sure you're on track, ask. For example, "Is this the type of
  information you had in mind?"
- Learn the personal and professional characteristics of the ideal candi-
  date.
- Ask questions to discover the history and current status of organiza-
  tional problems.
- Listen, listen, listen.

- Be a problem solver.

- Synthesize information to formulate suspected needs.

- Clarify information and ask the interviewer for help in confirming needs.

- *Be positive.*

Phase 3: Is There a Fit?

Interviewer's Agenda:

- Evaluate organizational fit

Candidate's Agenda:

- Present skills/abilities

The interviewer's concern, in this phase, is with that nebulous quality called fit. The interviewer is basically asking himself whether your personal style and management approach will work well in the company. Fit was defined earlier as trying to ascertain a match between the way the business is done (the environment, products, and services) and the values, integrity, and goals of the candidate. Many interviewers begin to get a feel for fit in the rapport building at the beginning of the interview.

One way interviewers might approach fit is by asking you to address specific business situations you have faced in your business career. They can have you describe a specific problem, your thought process in attacking the problem, the way you identified possible solutions, why the selected solution was chosen, and then the degree of success you attained. Interviewers are interested in how and why you made your decisions, and want to explore your thought process as fully as possible. It is important to allow them to pursue their line of questioning until they are satisfied, even if the amount of time on one topic seems endless to you. In a variation of this method, interviewers give you business situations and ask how you would handle each one.

Interviewers may prefer a third method, which is asking broad, conceptual questions to get a feel for fit. It is important for you to have thought about some of these questions prior to the interview. Being prepared makes you feel confident and creates clear, brief, and assured responses. A representative sample of possible interview questions follows:

- What are your three greatest accomplishments? Three greatest blunders? Explain them.

- What is your management style?

- How do you manage an overachiever? An underachiever?
- Describe the attributes of your best boss. Worst boss.
- Define the perfect relationship with a boss. Most difficult relationship.
- How did you grow personally and professionally in your last position?
- What relevance did your college course of study have to our position?
- Define the perfect job.
- What elements does a job need to give you satisfaction?
- What are three motivators? Three demotivators?
- What are your strengths? Weaknesses?
- What would your spouse and/or best friend say were your strengths? Weaknesses?
- What would you like to be doing three years from now?

As the candidate, your interest during this part of the interview is in presenting the skills and abilities that convince the interviewer that you are the best candidate. The wise use of time in making your presentation is critical to an efficient sell. You have limited time to make your points, which increases the importance of outstanding preparation. Let's examine this issue more closely to understand the time constraints you are dealing with.

Let's assume that you are successful in achieving your goal, and a 50–50 percent business conversation develops during the interview. Let's also assume an average interview length to be approximately an hour. Given that ten minutes are spent on rapport building and five minutes are spent on the close, approximately 45 minutes remain for the business portion of the meeting. Since only one-half of the 45 minutes might be yours, you are left with 20–25 minutes to ascertain information about the company, its goals, and its people, understand the needs, present your skills and abilities, raise concerns and resolve them, be involved in the close, and determine the next steps in the interviewing process.

However, that analysis makes a major assumption that the interviewer doesn't need any of the time allotted to you to attain the information needed to make a decision about hiring you. Throughout the book we have stated that interviewers are in a more favored status than the candidate; hence the need to accomplish their agendas first. So if interviewers need more time, they take it. Obviously it is in your best interest to let them.

Do these limitations seem a little overwhelming? They are if you are not completely prepared and cannot present things in a clear, crisp manner. Effective selling of your skills and abilities depends on three questions:

> **INTERVIEW TIP—COMPETENCIES/ACCOMPLISHMENTS**
>
> Present two to four of your strongest competencies and be prepared to defend them by citing bottom-line accomplishments.

1. Have you discovered and confirmed the real needs of the organization?

2. Have you prepared by identifying your best accomplishments to illustrate your key skills and abilities including bottom line results?

3. Have you practiced presenting the skills and abilities in an honest, straightforward manner with a smooth, organized delivery?

With these factors in place, time constraints are not intimidating.

Assertive candidates can employ another strategy in addition to using time wisely. It is preparing a *proposal of fit*. (This is our term; you call it anything you want.) This proposal helps the interviewer by analyzing how your skills can benefit the organization. The importance of the concept is that it is the candidate's responsibility to make this happen, not the interviewer's. Understanding where you might fit is a developmental process that becomes more complete as you learn more about the organization and meet more people. On the first interview, you may know only what you have been able to learn from library research. During that interview you learn more about the organization and where it is headed. As you move from the first interviewer to others (or to the same interviewer a second or third time), you may very possibly move forward during an interview and then slip back to square one (in terms of progress in the interviewer's head) between interviews. In fact, this is likely to happen if there is time between the interviews, because the interviewer forgets about you shortly after you leave the office and he goes back to work. When you come back to see him (or another interviewer), everyone has forgotten a lot about the last conversation, and you start over again.

As a business consultant who would like to complete a sale, your role is to analyze what you learned after an interview and determine how you can assist the company to achieve its goals. Then, when you have another interview, you are able to update the interviewer concerning prior discussions and indicate how you can help. Whether this is a defined opening with a clear job specification or a less clearly defined job creation makes no difference. In the former case you indicate how you could perform successfully in that position. In the latter you indicate how your skills would be helpful in area A, B, or C.

The proposal of fit strategy assists the interviewer to move the discussion forward and is helpful to you because it is based on your work and should afford you many opportunities to cite your successes. Let's consider the example of a clearly defined sales management position, in which the candidate is seeing another in a line of interviewers:

> INTERVIEWER: Have you discussed any of the specifics of our sales management needs in your prior interviews?
>
> CANDIDATE: I believe I have. There is a need for a take-charge sales manager who can handle the recruitment and hiring of quality staff and develop and implement effective evaluation policies.
>
> INTERVIEWER: Yes, that's right. Can you do all three?

This type of summary enables you to review prior meetings so that the conversation can move forward (from square three to five instead of slipping back to square one).

A different twist occurs when the company is considering creating a position. In this situation the candidate may have to generate ideas (verbally or in written form) that indicate where value could be added:

> INTERVIEWER: In your discussions with Tracy, did you discuss a specific position?
>
> CANDIDATE: No, but she has given me some ideas as to the organization's needs. I've gathered as much information as I can and have developed three new business ideas that could expand your product lines and add significantly to the bottom line.
>
> INTERVIEWER: I'd love to hear your ideas.
>
> CANDIDATE: I've prepared a brief outline. [*Note:* This should be on one side of a sheet of paper.]

A candidate who is crisp and to the point, uses time wisely, and helps the interviewer to move the discussion forward is likely to be successful. An additional benefit is that proactive candidates who are focused on how their skills and abilities can bring value to the company are much less likely to volunteer weaknesses. Candidates who are passive and reacting to questions are much more likely to be caught off-guard or ill prepared and volunteer weaknesses (often ones that are not even requested).

INTERVIEW TIP—CONSULTATION

Propose how you can help to solve the needs or how the organization can use your skills.

Tactics

- Make clear, crisp comments or answers to questions.
- Focus on the needs of the organization.
- Demonstrate how you can help solve the organization's problems.
- Defend your abilities with specific, bottom-line-oriented accomplishments.
- Use time wisely and efficiently.
- Project self-confidence (don't volunteer negatives).
- *Be positive.*

Phase 4: Resolve Interviewer's Concerns

Interviewer's Agenda:

- Sell candidate on company

Candidate's Agenda:

- Test candidacy
- Overcome concerns

By this stage in the process, the interviewer has a strong sense of whether you fit the bill and can offer another interview or the position. One last issue of concern to the interviewer is to ask about your weaknesses. It is critical for you to spend time preparing the best possible answer. Ideally, you want to apply the following guidelines:

1. The response must be truthful.
2. Speak about something that is not fatal to your candidacy.
3. Explain how you have overcome, or how you are working to overcome, the weakness.

An example might be, "I am driven and expect a great deal of my people." You have to be prepared for the interviewer to come back and ask if you are too hard on your people. You might say, "I believe that I have learned that motivation is an individual matter, and I am regarded as a demanding but fair boss." Another example occurred when we interviewed the general manager of a chemical plant. When asked a weakness he said, "I was not comfortable speaking before a large group, so I took a public speaking course. Then I was able to practice my public speaking skills while communicating with the staff."

During this phase of the meeting, interviewers normally talk about their organizations. When the candidate is being given strong consideration, the "sell" is enthusiastic and warm. Interviewers answer the candidate's questions fully and attempt to put the company in the best possible light while emphasizing the strengths of the organization. If you find yourself in this situation, enjoy it and use the time to learn more about the organization. This may also be a time when you can volunteer additional skills, abilities, or accomplishments to further your candidacy. Since the bonding process is continuing, you should do nothing to cut this process off.

In the alternative, if interviewers are not as sure whether you will continue in the process, you can probably tell. The answers to your questions are usually polite and short, without much additional information. If you really want this position, you have to make a serious attempt to overcome the interviewer's objections.

More likely, however, is the scenario where the interviewer perceives that you have the skills and abilities to do the job but isn't sure that you are a perfect fit. Indeed, few candidates are ever a perfect fit. This allows you the opportunity to test your candidacy and, if there are any concerns, to overcome them.

When someone thinks about raising and overcoming objections, it is often viewed as having to deal with real or perceived rejection. This isn't easy in any phase of life. It is tough when someone refuses to go out with you, when you lose an election, when the product you are selling doesn't sell, or when a volunteer organization you believe in can't attract donations. The rejection of the product or the service organization, however, is nowhere near as difficult to deal with as the personal rejection felt in the date or the election. This is you, your very fiber, and it really hurts. The rejection in an interview, even if you have asked for problems to be brought to the surface, can feel like a personal rejection because you are talking about yourself, your skills, your abilities, your accomplishments, *and* your weaknesses.

Why, then, would anyone go out to generate rejection? The answer is simple. Raising objections in an interview is not seeking rejection. Remember that you were screened before you ever got to the interview. You were deemed to be one of the best qualified of the applicants, or you would not have received an interview. Rejection is not associated with "best qualified."

Raising objections is a means of getting concerns out on the table while you're together. Then you have an opportunity to resolve them rather than leaving without knowing the concerns in the interviewer's head. Earlier, we discussed asking for the ideal candidate characteristics as a means of setting the groundwork for this topic. Now it is possible to ask, "Mr. Jones, earlier I asked about the ideal personal and professional characteristics you have targeted. I feel I am a strong match. Can you tell me your reaction to the fit?"

Concerns fall into two basic categories: those you can fix and those you can't fix. A "can't fix" concern could be that the candidate must be a lawyer (which you're not) or have an MBA (which you don't). A "can fix" concern is a comment like, "I'm not sure you have enough sales experience in your background." If most concerns fell in the can't fix category, we probably wouldn't raise the issue.

But that isn't the case. If you lacked a major skill set, you would never have been called in for an interview. Consequently, almost all concerns are in the "can fix" category, and the issue is one of clarification or explaining a skill set that hasn't been discussed in the interview. In response to the concern about sales experience you might say, "Mr. Jones, we haven't had a chance to discuss my three years' direct sales experience for X company [a consumer products company]...." Whether you need to clarify information or discuss a new skill set, it is a great opportunity for you. You're helping the interviewer learn more about your skills and abilities while clarifying misconceptions.

In addition, you have a unique opportunity to continue to build the relationship. Here is an opening to take a challenge, turn it to a positive that furthers your candidacy, and continue to build your relationship with the interviewer.

Strategy is an issue only to the extent that it is usually in your interest to resolve the interviewer's concerns as quickly as possible, then to encourage conversation when the discussion focuses on your skills and abilities. In short, you'd like the conversation to go on as long as possible when it is positive. When your style is open and confident in this part of the meeting, it encourages the interviewer to be objective and forthright, thereby giving you the best chance to be successful.

Tactics

- Ask the interviewer what concerns he has with your candidacy.

- Don't take objections personally.

- Approach objections or concerns as a major opportunity.

INTERVIEW TIP—OVERCOMING OBJECTIONS

Resolving a concern gives you a terrific opportunity to clarify something you said, to put forth additional skills, and to extend the interview.

- Continue the conversation as long as it is positive.
- Have an answer for, "What are your weaknesses?"
- Deal with perceived weaknesses from a positive point of view (i.e., how you have overcome the weakness or how are you working on it).
- Continue to gather data to evaluate the organization.
- *Be positive.*

Phase 5: Close the Interview with Enthusiasm

Interviewer's Agenda:

- Build rapport
- Close

Candidate's Agenda:

- Build rapport
- Close

Once the interviewer has accomplished his agenda, he may tell you about the next steps and close the meeting. Usually, the more he likes you, the more information you receive about upcoming events, such as additional interviews.

Openness and confidence should characterize your strategy for the close. This is a great opportunity to continue the bonding process with the interviewer. In addition, you have an opportunity to tell the interviewer anything else that you feel is important to your candidacy. Just knowing that you have this opportunity removes pressure during the interview. You want to thank the interviewer for taking the time to meet you, tell him about your excitement with the things he is doing (if you can say so truthfully), and understand the time and the process from this interview until the successful candidate is offered the job. Finally, if you are convinced that you would like to work for the company, indicate that enthu-

---

INTERVIEW TIP—ASK FOR THE JOB

Interviewing is no place for the timid. If you find a job you really want, and if you are qualified and well-prepared enough to get an interview, tell the interviewer you want to work for him.

siasm to the interviewer, especially if he is your potential boss. This is not a junior high school dance where it is in vogue to stand off and "be cool."

Tactics

- Tell the interviewer how excited you are about the possibility of working with him.
- Remember that, if the interviewer "loves you," anything is possible.
- Ask for the job.
- Understand the next steps in the interviewing process and the expected timeframes.
- Obtain information that will help you in the upcoming interviews.
- *Be positive.*

Summary

Within the interview framework, it is possible to implement strategies that increase the likelihood for success. Strategies must be used professionally and within the comfort zone of the interviewer. You are not trying to take the meeting over; rather, you are looking for a chance to accomplish your agenda as well as help the interviewer accomplish his. Key points of discussion are:

- Building rapport (by being approachable and interested and having fun) increases the chances of success.
- Consistently positive behavior in your presentation and content leaves a positive impression with the interviewer.
- A business discussion (50 percent talk each) is your best opportunity to accomplish your agenda.
- After selling your skills and abilities to solve the company's problems, ask for the job.

STEP 8

Evaluate Your Performance

Competitive interviewing requires the measurement of your progress against your objectives and should even occur during the interview.

Psychologists tell us we can remember only a limited number of things in short-term memory. Therefore, we have settled on the three basic objectives of Step 6:

- Build rapport
- Accomplish the interviewer's agenda
- Accomplish the candidate's agenda.

These objectives can be managed during the interview. Any more than this and your energy is focused on remembering objectives rather than on the interview.

Prior to the interview (for preparation and review) and after the interview (for evaluation), longer checklists, such as "Key Interview Tips" (Appendix A), can be helpful.

Immediately after the interview, the longer evaluation checklist of your performance, presented in this chapter, is of great value. It is helpful for at least two reasons. First, since people tend to be extremely self-critical, the objectivity of an evaluation tool helps to keep an interview in proper perspective. Often you realize that you did a better job than you thought. Second, complete self-assessment has a positive long-term effect. It immediately reinforces positive behaviors and points to necessary changes in negative behaviors.

Consequently, we recommend three tools:

- Prior to the interview, review the "Key Interview Tips" (Appendix A).
- During the interview, manage the information in "Short Evaluation (Three Basic Objectives)."
- After the interview, review the "Long Evaluation Checklist" in this chapter.

Short Evaluation
(Three Basic Objectives)

You need memorize only the three objectives. Since they are practical and simple, they become an integral part of your interview routine. A simple mental determination—"accomplished" or "not accomplished"—every so often during the interview gives you indication of where you are. A "not accomplished" indicates an opportunity. The mental score board (A = accomplished, NA = not accomplished) looks like this:

Objective 1: Recognize the importance of building rapport. Did we discover and discuss one or two common interests, acquaintances, or experiences?   A   NA

Objective 2: Accomplish the interviewer's agenda. Did the interviewer learn my two or three strongest competencies and did I support them with bottom-line accomplishments?   A   NA

Objective 3: Accomplish the candidate's agenda. Did I identify three or four of the organization's most critical needs, confirm them with the interviewer, and clearly sell my specific abilities to satisfy each need? A   NA

As you mentally check the scoreboard at various points in the meeting, you can gauge what you have to accomplish. Then, using the strategies and tactics discussed in the last chapter, you can make it happen. It's simple and it works.

Long Evaluation (Checklist)

After the interview, look at the three basic objectives and the criteria that comprise them. Evaluate the criteria one at a time using a ranking of 1 to 5 (5 being high).

Objective 1: Recognize the Importance of Building Rapport. Did we discover and discuss one or two common interests, acquaintances, or experiences?

Criteria 1
Personal Interaction

The interviewer made me feel comfortable.	1 2 3 4 5
I made the interviewer feel comfortable.	1 2 3 4 5
The interviewer smiled or laughed.	1 2 3 4 5
I smiled or laughed.	1 2 3 4 5
The interviewer was comfortable with herself.	1 2 3 4 5
The interviewer made eye contact.	1 2 3 4 5
I made eye contact.	1 2 3 4 5
The interviewer was open and sincere.	1 2 3 4 5
I was open and sincere with the interviewer.	1 2 3 4 5
I felt free to ask questions.	1 2 3 4 5
I was able to express my ideas openly.	1 2 3 4 5
We identified common interests.	1 2 3 4 5
We identified common friends or acquaintances.	1 2 3 4 5
We discussed common experiences.	1 2 3 4 5

Professional Issues

The interviewer seems to enjoy working for the company.	1 2 3 4 5
The interviewer seems to enjoy her job.	1 2 3 4 5
I would want to work for this person.	1 2 3 4 5
The interviewer was willing to give me information about the company (bad as well as good).	1 2 3 4 5

Building rapport is a two-way street. If the interviewer is comfortable with the process, she may take the lead. If not, it may fall to you to keep the conversation going. "Why me?" you might ask. "That's the interviewer's role." That may be true in a theoretical sense, but it is irrelevant in reality.

CAREER PROFILE
Assisting the Interviewer

It was obvious to Jorge, a candidate for a finance position, that Marge, his potential boss, was uneasy in her role as interviewer. Marge greeted Jorge stiffly after he had been brought to her office by her secretary. Marge sat behind the protection of her large desk peering over the top of a lot of files. Halting small talk lasted less than three minutes (it seemed like an hour) before Marge mercifully turned the discussion to business.

Jorge was wise enough to understand that rapport building is an ongoing theme throughout the interview. As the interview progressed, Jorge learned that Marge had been in her job less than a year and it was her first management position. Jorge felt that Marge seemed shy in addition to being uncomfortable with her responsibility to recruit and hire someone for this key position. Jorge was not very comfortable himself (who would be?), but he did his best to appear relaxed.

When Marge asked a question, Jorge tried to give a little extra detail in the hope of hitting a responsive chord and he tried to smile when appropriate. (*Note:* Marge later admitted that informal conversation was extremely difficult for her; so you can imagine how Jorge must have felt.) Finally, Marge asked Jorge a question about why he left a certain position. Jorge said, "My wife's father was ill and, since he was alone, Sue felt that she needed to be close to him. That required a move from Colorado back to Connecticut, so I resigned. Before we came back, however, we took three weeks to take one last white water rafting trip."

The last sentence that Jorge added could have been nothing more than a little color, but it was the one that lit up the scoreboard. Marge's expression changed, her eyes lit up, and she came alive. "You did white water rafting in Colorado?" she asked. "Yes," said Jorge, "on the Arkansas and the Colorado rivers. It was our favorite recreational activity." Marge loved the outdoors. She and her husband had done white water canoeing on most of the major rivers in the East and were planning their first trip to the West. Marge completely forgot her heavily structured interview (every question had been listed on a sheet of paper), and she wanted to know about rafting through the Grand Canyon. Jorge was happy to tell her about travel arrangements, places to stay, and the best guides. The conversation wasn't difficult anymore.

After thoroughly discussing her summer plans, Marge suggested that they return to the business discussion (Jorge would never have cut off the rafting discussion). Now, however, the interview became a relaxed business conversation rather than the uncomfortable question/answer format. Jorge asked as many questions of Marge and was able to focus his answers on her business concerns.

Jorge had a series of interviews with Marge's boss and others in Marge's department, but he felt that he had won the job in that interview when the discussion turned to white water rafting. Marge later verified that his feeling was correct. She said that she was scared to death hiring her first key person and Jorge not only had the necessary skills but helped her to overcome her nervousness. His patience and concern for the interviewer's comfort won the day. ❑

Objective 2: Accomplish the Interviewer's Agenda. Did the interviewer learn my two or three strongest competencies and did I support them with bottom-line accomplishments?

Criteria 2

Personal/Professional Skills

I was direct and to the point.	1 2 3 4 5
The interviewer appeared to be satisfied that I specifically and concisely answered the questions.	1 2 3 4 5
I have the following evidence to support that assessment. _____	
I followed the basic principle that no answer should be longer than 60 seconds.	1 2 3 4 5
The interviewer did not have to clarify or repeat many questions.	1 2 3 4 5
I cited skills and abilities that were relevant to the job needs.	1 2 3 4 5
The interviewer gained a clear picture of my strongest personal and professional skills.	1 2 3 4 5
My examples were bottom-line-oriented.	1 2 3 4 5
I demonstrated my ability to learn new skills quickly.	1 2 3 4 5
I gave strong examples of my flexibility and adaptability.	1 2 3 4 5
My leadership and management skills were discussed.	1 2 3 4 5

A real concern in the interview occurs right after the transition from rapport building to the business portion of the meeting. You need to help the interviewer attain a comfort level even if it means holding back on your agenda for more time than feels comfortable. Richard put himself in a difficult position on just this issue.

Reading the Cues

Richard was interviewing with Sylvia for a marketing position. Rapport building had gone smoothly. The discussion was conversational in tone and very relaxed. It was clear to Richard that Sylvia liked him.

As Sylvia made the transition to the business portion of the meeting, Richard was feeling very confident. Things had been so relaxed to this point that he was sure he'd be able to get Sylvia to talk about the business needs of her department. He made the fatal mistake of assuming that a relaxed, conversational style in the rapport building phase would automatically carry over to the initial phases of the business meeting. Instead of assisting Sylvia to reach a comfort level, he tried to get at her business needs too early. When he started to ask her questions before she was ready, she reverted to a typical question/answer style, which signaled to him that she was uncomfortable with his behavior. Fortunately, he immediately realized what he had done. He had lost sight of helping Sylvia with her agenda in an effort to accomplish his own agenda.

At this point he had lost most of the rapport he had developed earlier. Rather than push further he just followed Sylvia's lead. When she asked questions about his accomplishments, Richard kept his answers short because he realized that he had not yet let her completely cover her needs. As time went on, she began to become more comfortable again. By the last one-third of the meeting they were involved in an intense business discussion. Sylvia told Richard the major needs of her department and, sure enough, they were different from what Richard's intelligence had provided. He was pleased that he had kept his answers short. Now that he knew the real needs, he was able to target his accomplishments to Sylvia's needs.

When he left the interview, Richard was upset with himself. He should have known better than to press too soon. Yet, on the positive side, he had seemed to save the day. He mentally gave himself a B for the interview (it would have been an A except for the major error in judgment). Needless to say, he felt a lot better three interviews later when he was hired.   ❑

"How I was able to help the interviewer?" is in many ways the most difficult objective to self-evaluate. How do you know whether you are focusing on the interviewer's interests? To get at this, you have to focus on the things you can control, such as your ability to listen, to respond to a question, to give clear answers, and to keep the answers short.

Objective 3: Accomplish the Candidate's Agenda. Did I identify three or four of the organization's most critical needs, confirm them with the interviewer, and clearly sell my specific abilities to satisfy each need?

Criteria 3

Identify Needs

Each of us spoke about 50 percent of the time in each phase of the interview.	1 2 3 4 5
I was comfortable asking questions.	1 2 3 4 5
The questions generated needs.	1 2 3 4 5
The questions were insightful and were a natural outgrowth of the conversation.	1 2 3 4 5
The interview remained in an easy, give-and-take conversational style.	1 2 3 4 5

Confirm Needs

I confirmed the organization's needs.	1 2 3 4 5
I was able to generate additional needs during this portion of the meeting.	1 2 3 4 5
My initial hunches concerning needs were correct.	1 2 3 4 5

Sell Abilities

I was clear and concise in my presentation.	1 2 3 4 5
I maintained the interviewer's interest as I presented my skills and abilities.	1 2 3 4 5
The interviewer was interested and involved.	1 2 3 4 5
I cited statistics that demonstrated how my contributions impacted the bottom line.	1 2 3 4 5
I told the interviewer I wanted to work for her.	1 2 3 4 5
I asked for the job.	1 2 3 4 5

We have spoken a good deal about the process, but it is also extremely important to maintain sight of the objective. Anna forgot that she was interviewing with an extremely aggressive group of people; consequently, she needed to express how much she wanted to work with them and to ask for the job.

CAREER PROFILE
Asking for the Job

Anna knew exactly what she wanted to happen in her interview for a marketing job in a consumer products company. The personal interaction with Carter, the product manager, had been pleasant and included a number of friends and common interests. Smiles and a relaxed flow defined the conversation. When Carter changed the focus to business, he continued in the same relaxed style. When Anna realized that she was able to generate business needs, she felt confident. The conversation was a 50–50 percent business discussion from the start. "Perfect—this meeting is going so well," she thought. After generating and clarifying needs, the conversation turned to what the company was doing to solve them. The remainder of the meeting seemed to be a textbook case of how to conduct an interview. When she left, Anna rated herself an A.

When she received the rejection letter two weeks later, she was irate. She called Carter immediately but he was not in. She called him every other day for two weeks. Finally, she got him on the telephone at six o'clock one evening. Blunt and honest, she said, "I thought we had a great interview. I couldn't believe the rejection letter." Surprisingly, Carter was as blunt, saying:

> Look, I really liked you. You have a great background, went to all the right schools, and your prior experience was terrific. But I work in an aggressive, competitive environment, and your style showed me none of that. You developed needs and confirmed them, but you never told me what you were going to do to help me solve them. You'd never survive in this climate as a wallflower. And you never told me you wanted the job or asked me for it. So I didn't give it to you. It was as simple as that.

Anna couldn't believe what she had done. She had followed the process up until the sell and the close. She knew that, to achieve the outcome she wanted, she needed to be aggressive and she had not been. She got lulled to sleep and she lost sight of her full agenda.

In addition, she realized that she had lost a huge opportunity with someone like Carter, who was a candid and open communicator. If, during the interview, she had asked, "Am I on track?" Carter probably would have given her signals, either verbal or nonverbal, that would have screamed out at her:

> Anna, you're not here merely to make the interviewing process work as well as the X's and O's on a coach's blackboard. You're here to get a job and I am an aggressive guy, in an aggressive company, in an aggressive industry. Despite the style I am using to conduct the interview, you'd better show some aggressiveness in accomplishing your objectives and then test to see how you're doing.

But she hadn't and she lost. For about three days she licked her wounds. As she replayed the final conversation with Carter in her mind, she remembered he had clearly said that he didn't give her the job because she didn't ask for it. However, he didn't say that he had hired anyone else. "Maybe," Anna thought, "it's not too late." She called Carter's secretary and leveled with her about what had happened. Anna asked whether the position had been filled. The answer that came back was "no," but Carter was seeing a lot of people and was close to a decision.

Anna knew she couldn't wait. Once before she had been lucky late in the afternoon so she called again around six o'clock. Carter picked up the phone. When he discovered it was Anna he tried to be courteous, but it was clear he wanted to get her off the phone. This time, however, Anna was very clear on her outcome goals. She was extremely precise about how she could help Carter with specific examples of aggressive accomplishments and she completed her sales presentation in about 90 seconds. She told Carter that her goal had been 60 seconds and she apologized for the additional 30 seconds. Her agenda was clear: interview me again. He did. She was offered the job, and accepted it.   ❏

Summary

Evaluation is most productive if it is accomplished during the interview. A simple mental assessment at various points during the interview helps you to assess how you are progressing. If you need a course correction, you can utilize the appropriate strategies and tactics to accomplish your goals. The objectives are:

Objective 1: Recognize the importance of building rapport. Did we discover and discuss one or two common interests, acquaintances, or experiences?

Objective 2: Accomplish the interviewer's agenda. Did the interviewer learn my two or three strongest competencies and did I support them with bottom-line accomplishments?

Objective 3: Accomplish the candidate's agenda. Did I identify three or four of the organization's most critical needs, confirm them with the interviewer, and clearly sell my specific abilities to satisfy each need?

Prior to the interview, a review of the "Key Interview Tips" (Appendix A) can be beneficial. After the interview, the in-depth analysis presented in this chapter can serve to reinforce your positive behaviors and assist with course corrections for the next interview.

PART 4

Selecting the Right Company

STEP 9

Appraise the Company

The buy side of the equation is often neglected, in whole or in part, by prospective job seekers. The premise of the buy side study goes like this: "As a prospective employee, I have as much responsibility to judge and evaluate prospective employers as they do to judge and evaluate me. If the employer and I both do our jobs well, we both enhance the likelihood of achieving a great match." The reason for needing to make a good decision is clear. There is only a finite number of career decisions and/or moves to make during the course of a business career.

Most people agree that they are happier, more content, and easier to live with when:

- They are in a challenging job.
- Their company is doing well.
- They work with bright, stimulating, and fun people.
- They can visualize a career path.

Any time that someone is in the process of changing jobs, companies, or careers, their normal life equilibrium is temporarily thrown out of balance. The imbalance can last a short time if a good career choice is made or a long time if a poor choice is made. Not only can a poor choice make you unhappy, but it can also hold you at the same level or actually move your career backward, thus making future moves more difficult. Obviously, no one wants that to happen. That's why the buy side of the decision is so important.

The buy side analysis is concerned with three major topics: company, position, and people. If your scorecard gives high marks in all of these areas, then you will most likely be happy and successful in the position. For each of these three areas, a case study is presented and a methodology or scorecard for evaluating a position is examined.

CAREER PROFILE
Company

Josh was 46 years old, married, and the father of two children. He had spent his entire working career in the same pharmaceutical company and was currently vice-president for manufacturing. He had a Ph.D. in chemical engineering and had started his career in research. After a number of years in the lab, he moved briefly to marketing and then to manufacturing where he found his niche. Josh had been extremely happy during most of his working career, but more recently he had been having some problems.

As he sat in management meetings he found his ideas and reactions were frequently headed in a different direction than those of other members of the senior management team. He gradually felt angry and frustrated. He tried to determine why by talking with colleagues and doing some soul searching. The company, while profitable, was not doing as well as it had ten years earlier. Since revenue was not increasing fast enough, this translated into cost-cutting measures. For a period of time, Josh thought this was a productive and healthy process for the organization. There was no doubt that there were excesses in all areas of the organization's budget, the remnants of the "good old days."

Josh initially felt good about his role in the process as he helped the company position itself for the next century. As time went on, however, a second and a third round of cost cutting were initiated, Josh found himself at odds with the other managers. He felt that the cuts had gone beyond the fat and now were cutting into the bone.

He had always held to extremely high standards in the manufacturing process. He demanded the procurement of the best supplies and materials, and he had consistently produced an outstanding product. It had been Josh's trademark and that of the company. Through the years his concern with quality had been praised by senior management and had also been the target of a good-natured joke now and then. Now, Josh's philosophy was being threatened by the new cost-cutting policies and he didn't like it. His arguments and appeals for a reasonable cost-cutting attitude that would not impact the quality of the product seemed to fall on deaf ears.

Josh went through an agonizing period of time trying to decide on his course of action. He didn't want to leave the company but he tried to look at both the emotional and the financial issues. He spoke with his wife, who finally put the whole thing in perspective when she said, "Josh, there is no job worth what you are putting yourself through. These people don't seem to care about a quality product anymore and you do. If you stay and bat your head against a wall, you are going to make yourself sick. So get out." The words cut to the heart of the matter. Josh thought about them and decided to leave.

His job search took some time because he was still fully employed, but after four months he had two very active and very different leads. The first lead was very much in the mold of what he had been doing. It was a vice-president for manufacturing position with a pharmaceutical firm slightly smaller than his present company. Josh had done some checking with friends and business associates, and in general the company was not held in as high regard as his present company. The issues with the company, as they related to manufacturing, centered on a lack of product consistency. With the present circumstances clear in his mind, all sorts of red flags waved in Josh's mind. He was ready to walk away from the opportunity until he heard that there was a new senior management team.

After meeting the new team, he began to rethink his concerns. The president seemed to be very open when he admitted that the company had been experiencing problems and, although costs had to be managed, product quality was of major concern to him. He was told that the vice-president for manufacturing would be a key person on the president's staff and would be expected to contribute a great deal. Josh liked the senior managers. He felt they were sincere and he thought their views of the business made sense.

Josh didn't like everything the president had to say about compensation and benefits, because this was an area where costs would be closely monitored, but it seemed to make sense. He said that he wanted to pay for results, not potential, so his philosophy was to pay less in salary and more in bonus. In Josh's case, he thought his salary might be 10 to 15 percent less than his current income, but it could be more than made up in bonus if the targets were hit. The company had just installed a "flex benefit" program that was designed to provide choices in benefit coverage. It also cost the company less and the employee a little more. There was no car, as had been the case in his present position. Josh was coming face to face with what he had been reading—a leaner, more cost-conscious approach to managing a business. The president explained that his hope was to keep expenses in line and to reward excellence.

The second opportunity that he uncovered was a new venture. Two doctors, who had worked for one of the most prestigious pharmaceutical firms in the area, had developed and patented two new drugs. The company was formed, the management team was being created, and a vice-president for manufacturing was the last piece that was needed. The risk/reward curve on this job was something that Josh had only read about. On the one hand, the business could be bankrupt in a year if the products didn't sell or something went wrong. In that case, Josh knew he would be looking for another job without the benefit of a severance package. On the other hand, the business could become a viable entity. In that case he would benefit because he would receive large increases in salary and bonus, and he would receive equity in the company. Although the initial salary would be about 20 percent less than in his current job, there was clearly great potential if the company succeeded.

Josh continued to interview with both firms. The environment with the pharmaceutical company was comfortable. He understood the work and knew he could perform successfully, but he felt some insecurity about the company's position in the industry. What was helping him overcome his concerns was that he felt the new management was first class. He believed that they wanted to turn the situation around. The start-up with the doctors, on the other hand, was perplexing. It was the antithesis of everything Josh had ever done. The doctors were financially solvent but things would be extremely tight in the beginning. It would be a real shirt sleeve operation with everyone pitching in and doing whatever was necessary to propel the organization. Each person's contribution would be extremely meaningful, and there would be a "create it as you go" philosophy rather than a "follow the procedure" mentality. Josh didn't know how he would react to such conditions. Despite his reservations, however, there was something very intriguing about being part of the birth of an organization and building something. Josh really liked the doctors and the management team, and he felt he would enjoy working with them.

To help make a decision, he listed the pluses and minuses of the jobs (since he liked the people equally well and he could perform the work successfully, he left those items off the list), which looked like this:

Company	Plus	Minus
Pharmaceutical	■ New management ■ Established company ■ Track record ■ Higher salary	■ General reputation ■ Position in industry ■ Possibility of same problems
New Venture	■ Start-up ■ Exciting ■ Teamwork ■ Higher risk	■ Is business viable? ■ No track record ■ Are doctors good businesspeople? ■ Lower salary

In another three weeks Josh landed offers from both companies. He was justifiably proud since it had been so long since he last interviewed. He considered the pluses and minuses of his decision until he couldn't add any new thoughts to the equation.

Each time he thought about the positions, he tried to convince himself that the established company was the only sound choice. It was, after all, what he had done and he knew he could be successful. Of course, this company could get into trouble and begin to institute controls similar to his present company. The more he thought about his choices, the more excited he became about the start-up. It would obviously be different from anything he had done, and he would probably be scared to death some of the time. But here was an opportunity to be in on the ground floor of something, to help create something. To his amazement, his wife said that she was coming to the same conclusion. She asked that he conduct one more round of discussions with the doctors as a final check. After several more meetings he was more excited than ever and felt that any doubt had been erased. With great excitement and enthusiasm, Josh accepted the doctors' offer. ❑

CAREER PROFILE
Position

Erica was ecstatic. She had just received her second job offer. It was all the more rewarding since the financial markets were considered so bad at the time. The euphoria was short-lived, however, because she had to go about the process of making a decision. As she was walking home from the train station, she thought about her career history.

She had done a lot in 28 years. She had a B.A. in psychology and an MBA from excellent institutions. She had been recruited by one of the best money center banks to work in the aggressive deal origination area with emphasis on Latin America. This was due, in part, to her fluency in Spanish and Portuguese. She completed a successful run of three years as an associate due to her competitive nature and drive to move up in the organization. At that point an executive search consultant recruited her to another firm as a vice-president structuring financial deals in the energy industry. These were usually power plants or capital equipment. Erica enjoyed the job and learned a great many new skills. The major drawback was that the company was located in the suburbs outside the city and the reverse commute was difficult.

To compound the problem, Erica had been evaluating her life and career and they were coming into conflict. Earlier in her career, she found herself in hotel rooms in Latin America instead of gatherings with friends in New York. Now she found herself outside the city or traveling rather than having a chance to socialize. She didn't like this, nor did the new lover in her life.

Finally, Erica reached the point of deciding it was time to make a move back to the city. She conducted her search efficiently, looking for corporate finance or structured finance positions. Her expertise in the energy industry was considered a plus. Then, a curious thing happened. A friend in the executive search field recommended her to the head of cash management services at a high-quality, money center bank. This job clearly did not fit the profile of her job objective. However, in deference to her friend, Erica went to talk with Tom.

The position was one of selling cash management services. Tom, who had come from a corporate finance position, was honest and open with Erica. "Selling cash management services is not considered as high profile as structuring energy deals," Tom said. "However," he went on, "we are a profitable and important component of the bank." As they spoke, Erica gained a greater appreciation for the cash management area. She also discovered that the hours would not be as long as previously, and there would be less travel. On the flip side, although the base salary was about the same as before, her bonus potential would be substantially lower.

Erica had a number of additional interviews with people in Tom's group. She learned more about the group and the people. She was as honest with Tom as he had been with her. Erica indicated that her need for the meetings was to learn as much as possible about the work so that she could make an informed decision. Tom was extremely supportive of Erica's needs.

While this was happening, Erica received a call from a foreign conglomerate. They were interested in a start-up group assisting their customers to finance energy plants and capital equipment. They needed a controller for the group and Erica's background fit the bill. The fact that she had previous energy experience was her "value added." The corporation had finance people but none with energy experience.

The pluses to this job were clear. It would keep her in the fast track doing high-profile work since the department would be highly visible. Although her base salary would be the same as in the cash management position, her bonus potential would be a great deal higher. On the negative side, the hours would be long (perhaps extremely long) due to the nature of the work and the fact that it was a start-up.

The offer for the cash management position came first. Erica was able to buy ten days to make her decision. She called to see where she stood on the controllership. That call set the wheels in motion for a series of interviews in the short span of three days. At the end of that series of interviews Erica received an offer.

She clearly had some deep thinking to do. In her case, the people and the companies were of the highest quality. Her decision would come down to position and lifestyle. Her scratch notes looked like this:

Position	Plus	Minus
Cash Management	▪ Limited (10-hour) workday ▪ Evenings free ▪ Weekends free ▪ Time for friends	▪ Challenging work? ▪ Full use of my abilities? ▪ Less visibility ▪ Less compensation

Project Finance	■ Challenging work	■ 12- to 14-hour workdays
	■ Learn new skills	■ Heavy travel
	■ High visibility	■ Weekend work
	■ Great compensation potential	■ Little time for personal things

When Erica sat down to evaluate the cash management and project finance positions, her dilemma was clear. She could remain on the fast track in a highly visible, challenging position with high compensation, or she could move to a slightly slower track (most people would feel that a 10-hour day is still plenty fast enough) that would have less visibility and less compensation but with a dramatically improved lifestyle.

For a few days her thoughts seesawed. "Will the work be challenging? What will my friends think of me if I move to a cash management position? Will I end up in hotel rooms again in far away places on Saturday nights?" (Note: Erica considered that thought a nightmare.) "What if the cash management work isn't challenging? If the time commitment for project finance is long under normal circumstances, how much worse can it be in a start-up venture?" Her thoughts reached one conclusion and then another.

After much soul searching, Erica came to the conclusion that she wanted to try a change in her lifestyle so she accepted the cash management position. She knew that she had a fairly narrow window of time (perhaps a year or two) to decide if she truly enjoyed cash management after which she would probably not be able to go back to project finance. She was quite sure, however, that would be ample time to make a decision on the long-term merits of cash management. She enthusiastically accepted the position.   ❏

CAREER PROFILE
People

Lewis had been a salesperson for consumer food products all of his 15-year career. The Fortune 500 company where he worked had always demonstrated a "cradle to grave" mentality. In exchange for unquestioning loyalty, an employee could expect lifetime employment. Lewis had concerns about the nine moves that he had put his family through in the last 15 years, but at least they had all been in the Midwest where his entire family had been born and raised.

Lewis' career had been a slow but steady rise, which fit the company mold perfectly. His most recent position had been a promotion to manage a small sales office in Ohio. The concept of accepting a variety of assignments, in addition to a number of geographic locations, was also part of the company culture. The problem was that no one realized that this last move was not a good one for Lewis. The company fell on difficult times caused by poor management decisions, increased competition, and a recession. Hard decisions had to be made. A number of small sales offices had to be closed. Lewis' was one of them even though its productivity had been good by company standards. The company offered Lewis another position but it was a move back to sales in a location that was not desirable. Lewis' only alternative was to opt for a severance package. Ultimately, he accepted the package and left.

Lewis quickly got in control of his job campaign, and he and his wife made some decisions about where they wanted to live. The greater Chicago area was their first choice and St. Louis was also high on the list. Lewis began a job search for a sales management position. Lewis conducted an extremely efficient job campaign and within a number of months had identified two leads, one in the Chicago area and one in St. Louis. The leads turned into job offers within days of one another.

Each of the companies was involved in the sales of consumer food products and in each case Lewis was offered a sales management position. Lewis spent time in the library researching each company. From what he could learn, each company had been in business for a number of years, held a stable market share, and had solid management. Lewis continued a series of dialogs he had been having with friends in the industry to see if he could learn anything that would substantially influence his thinking about either of the companies. The feedback indicated that they were substantially the same.

Lewis and his family spent time discussing location. The difference in the locations was not considered to be a factor. Either was fine. In either case, there was a strong possibility that the company might move him and his family, although each company was reconsidering this strategy because of the prohibitive costs involved.

The two positions were substantially the same. In each case Lewis was to be a district sales manager. The offices were approximately the same size and he was surprised that he would have exactly the same number of professionals reporting to him. Even the budgets for the offices were almost identical to one another.

The decision was clearly not going to depend on either company or position. It would come down to the people and Lewis felt comfortable with the senior management at each of the companies. He was not sure how he was going to make his decision when a friend suggested that he go back and meet some additional people at each firm. After sleeping on the idea for a night Lewis decided the suggestion made a lot of sense. He called each company to ask for permission to visit the office he would manage. The Chicago firm immediately responded "Yes," and, in fact, said that they had been thinking of inviting Lewis to come to visit the office. The St. Louis firm was much more reluctant to have Lewis visit, and said they would have to talk it over and call him back. Eventually, they called and established a meeting at another location in St. Louis. They said they would have Lewis meet some of the people from the office at this off-site location. Lewis, needless to say, felt much better about the way the Chicago firm handled the situation.

Lewis visited the Chicago firm first. He was met by his prospective boss and they spent some time together. Then he met individually with three employees of the office. Lewis asked one of the people why the former sales manager had left the position. "He didn't reach his objectives," the person responded. Lewis pursued the subject further. It turned out that the manager had over 20 years with the company and he had risen from the sales ranks. Later, when Lewis was back with his potential boss he again asked about the former sales manager. Although the words were slightly different, the response was essentially the same. "He was a nice person and a good employee," the boss said. "However, after his children graduated from college he didn't seem to be driven with the same fire." The boss went on to explain that he had been given a fair severance package. Beyond that, there seemed to be some reluctance to talk about him.

The remainder of Lewis' visit went well. He met everyone in the office and they all seemed friendly and professional. There seemed to be a positive attitude about the company, the working environment, and each other. As Lewis left he felt very positive about the situation. He was a little disturbed about the way the former sales manager was handled, but he felt that perhaps he might feel different if he knew all the facts.

As he traveled to the St. Louis firm he had a concern about the reluctance of management to allow him to visit the office. When he arrived he was met by his potential boss and they spent a few hours together discussing the company, the state of the business, the strengths and weaknesses of the organization, and their objectives for next year. The boss told Lewis that the reason they could not take him to the office was because Arthur, the sales manager, was still in the position. He spent time telling Lewis about the decision to replace Arthur.

"Our policy," he said, "is not to remove anyone without giving them every opportunity to improve." He went on to explain that Arthur had progressed through the ranks to a sales management position where he had been quite productive. Then things started to deteriorate at work at about the same time as his marriage of 25 years fell apart. Over the period of 12 months the productivity in his office had deteriorated at the same rate as Arthur's individual productivity. Management then sat down with Arthur and put him on notice concerning his performance. A series of measurable objectives had been defined and Arthur signed off on them. It was now six months later and the office had not achieved any of the objectives. The boss shared Arthur's objectives with Lewis, and they seemed challenging but reasonable.

Lewis asked what the company planned to do with Arthur. The boss indicated that due to his longevity, Arthur would be offered one last chance to begin again as a salesperson in a different territory. The reason, he indicated, was that senior management believed that Arthur still had the ability to sell. Then, if he was able to regroup, he could again be considered for promotion to a sales management position. In the alternative, if Arthur did not accept the transfer, he would be given a severance package and released.

Lewis asked why the company had decided against promoting from within. In this case, he was told, the office had been neglected for a period of time and the decision was made to bring in new blood. In addition, although there was one person who might be interested in the job, management didn't think she was ready to assume the responsibility at this time.

Lewis was told that Arthur was not going to be informed until the new management was ready to move into place. However, three key people had been made aware so that they could meet with Lewis. Two of them were salespeople and one was the senior secretary of the office. Lewis then spent about an hour with each of those people. He was impressed with how caring each of them was toward Arthur and his situation. He was also impressed with the fact that each person defended management's stance that a change had to be made. Lewis asked one person whether everyone in the office would feel that way. "No," came the reply, a few people will argue that Arthur has been treated inequitably. But if they were to assess the situation objectively, they would determine that management had been fair—and maybe—more than fair." The remainder of Lewis' visit went well. He very much liked the three people he met and although he wanted to see the office and meet some more of the people he understood why it wasn't possible. He closed the day with a brief summary with his potential boss.

When Lewis arrived home he thought some more about the people in the two companies. Here were his thoughts:

People	Plus	Minus
Chicago	■ Congenial people ■ Made me comfortable ■ Very good situation	■ Senior management somewhat indifferent to someone in trouble ■ Management values less close to mine
St. Louis	■ Congenial people ■ Made me comfortable ■ Management values agree with mine ■ Excellent situation	■ Not able to go to the office itself ■ Not able to meet everyone in the office

Lewis was surprised at how effectively the visit had helped him come to terms with a very tough decision. He honestly believed that he could be effective and enjoy himself in either of the situations. Yet the visit had clearly shown him that one company dealt with its people in a manner that was more consistent with his values. His decision became clear and he accepted the position in St. Louis.   ❏

The Evaluation Process

As a potential buyer, you need to approach the buy side analysis with the same direction and purpose as you did in selling yourself into the job. Analysis needs to take place in each component of the potential position. You need to determine that the company is sound and that the environment meets its description, that the position represents the right challenge, that it is possible to be successful, and that the people are individuals with whom you want to associate. Having examined three case studies representing the three major areas of concern, you can formulate a set of questions to help you evaluate a given offer. The steps involve (1) having clear goals, (2) a method to gather data, and (3) a definition of the areas of focus.

The Goals

During the preparation stage of the job campaign, we discussed formulating an ideal job statement to set a target or a goal. With that statement as a sounding board, the opportunity (including the company, position, and people) can be assessed. Part of your assessment is to select a situation in which you can perform your work with success and enjoyment. Those who trust a situation on face value may well be setting themselves up for an unhappy experience and a poor career choice. Often it is not just you with something at stake, but members of your family as well.

Methodology

With the goals clear, the next question you must ask is, "What method should be employed?" The information gathering and analysis techniques you perform in evaluating a potential employer are much the same as those employed by a good company evaluating an acquisition candidate. In many respects this evaluation process is like the due diligence that is done prior to an acquisition.

Your task is to gather as much information as possible about specific areas of focus from sources that have direct or indirect (preferably direct) knowledge about the company and its people. This information, synthesized and evaluated, provides the data for an informed decision.

The sources of information are varied. Interviews with management and employees of the potential company are one way. This is obvious but the key to success is to ask penetrating questions. Networking contacts with friends or friends of friends who may have knowledge of the company or the industry are another source. Yet another consists of bankers, audit firm partners/management, investment bankers, attorneys, executive search consultants, or others who may be serving the company.

There are also numerous sources of written communication. Internal information published by the company may be helpful. Depending on the position being considered, it may be appropriate to request reports, copies of strategic plans, business plans, budgets, and other financial reports. External information published by the company can also be relevant, including annual reports, press releases, 10Ks (financial reports), quarterly reports, and proxy statements. Additional external material can be found in newspaper or magazine articles or in investment analyst research reports published about the company and its industry.

Another source of information is a visit to company facilities. A personal visit adds to your education about the company and almost always uncovers new and interesting information or perspective on the company. If you are outgoing, company employees are more friendly and helpful than you might expect.

Areas of Focus

With your goals and methodology clearly defined, you can evaluate three major areas of focus: the company, position, and people. The end result is a collection of data that helps you to make a judgment whether to accept or reject the job offer.

It is also possible to quantify the decision (in case you are evaluating more than one offer). You can assign a value of 1 (low) to 5 (high) for some of the questions. (*Note:* Within each section you will find some questions that are better answered by comments rather than by a numerical rating.) After answering the questions under "Company" you can tally the scores to evaluate where the company falls on the continuum from unhealthy (1.0 average) to extremely healthy (5.0 average). Questions under "Position" and "People" fall on the continuum from poor fit (1) to excellent fit (5) in the same manner. After obtaining averages for each set, you can obtain a composite score by averaging the scores for each major area.

Company

Identifying a healthy company has to be high on your list of priorities. You want to know that this company will be functioning one year, three years, and five years from now. If you're not sure whether it will be functioning, you have to assess whether your capabilities can help to direct the company onto the right course.

Although you don't have to have a financial background, you should examine the company's financial information to see whether the company is growing, remaining static, or declining. The balance sheet indicates the funding levels (debt and cash flow). You need to examine the company's strengths and weaknesses versus those of the competition to ascertain some relative position within the industry. The strength of the management team and the issue of management succession need to be examined. You should understand the ownership situation and understand any potential changes in ownership. Finally, you need to see if there are any regulatory threats to the company and how it views its social responsibility.

A. *Performance of the Overall Industry*

Has the industry been growing over the last five years? 1 2 3 4 5

Nationally? 1 2 3 4 5

Internationally (if relevant)? 1 2 3 4 5

Is the outlook positive?   1 2 3 4 5

What are the reasons for the trend? _____

B. *Performance Versus the Competition*

How would you rate the company's market share?   1 2 3 4 5

Has the market share been growing?   1 2 3 4 5

Who are the winners among the competition? _____

Is the company considered one of the best?   1 2 3 4 5

What positives and negatives can happen to change
the future of the company? _____

C. *Financial Performance of the Company*

How would you rate the most recent five years
of sales?   1 2 3 4 5

Operating profits?   1 2 3 4 5

After-tax profits?   1 2 3 4 5

Cash generation?   1 2 3 4 5

Are the trends positive?   1 2 3 4 5

What are the reasons for the trends? _____

What are the company's future projections on sales
and profits? _____

Are they credible?   1 2 3 4 5

How does actual performance in the most recent
year compare with budget or forecast?   1 2 3 4 5

How does the company's return on investment
compare with others in the industry?   1 2 3 4 5

How about return on sales (net income as a
percentage of sales)?   1 2 3 4 5

How does the price/earnings ratio of the company's
stock compare with that of competitors?   1 2 3 4 5

Note: Not all companies perform well at all times, especially in economic downturn. A good test of the management team is to look at what course they're taking in the face of adversity. If profits are declining, what programs are being implemented to control costs and improve productivity? If cash generation has been weak, what types of programs have been implemented to control working capital (inventories and receivables) and capital spending?

D. *Balance Sheet Issues*

Is the debt level reasonable?   1 2 3 4 5

How does it compare percentagewise to other
companies in the industry?   1 2 3 4 5

How do the interest/principal payments required
compare to the company's operating profit?   1 2 3 4 5

Is the company in violation of any bank covenants?   1 2 3 4 5

What are the company's plans to fund cash
requirements dictated by future growth plans
(i.e., capital spending, new product development,
and acquisitions)?   1 2 3 4 5

Has the company generated equity through public
offerings in the past?   1 2 3 4 5

How strong are its banking relationships?   1 2 3 4 5

E. *Ownership and Potential Changes to Ownership*

Is the company public or private? _____

If private, what are the objectives of the
owners? _____

If public, is the company widely or narrowly held? _____

If the stock price has fallen recently, is the company
a takeover target? _____

How will an ownership change affect the company
and the position in question? _____

F. *Management Succession*

Are the ages of key members of the management
team balanced?   1 2 3 4 5

Are backups in place?   1 2 3 4 5

Does the company have an active management
development program?   1 2 3 4 5

G. *Social Responsibility*

Are the company's policies regarding the
community sound and responsible?   1 2 3 4 5

Environmental responsibilities?   1 2 3 4 5

Health and safety practices?   1 2 3 4 5

Are there regulatory threats facing the company?   1 2 3 4 5

H. *Legal Issues*

Are there any major claims against the company that could impact its growth plans?	1 2 3 4 5
Does the company hire outstanding legal counsel?	1 2 3 4 5

Position

Having interesting and enjoyable work to do is often listed as number 1 on job satisfaction indices. The importance of meaningful work has been well documented. The lists contain things like association and friendship, purposeful activity, a feeling of personal worth, recognition, intrinsic enjoyment of the work, achievement and accomplishment, and economic reward among others. All these relate to having interesting work.

Not surprisingly, if you are in a position that affords you the correct level and degree of challenge and if you are successful, then your sense of self-worth rises as you achieve. And while you are successful, your self-confidence remains high, and the chances are good that you are regarded as successful in the organization. As that happens a whole series of positive things occur. Not only do you feel good about yourself and your peers feel good about you, but your boss and senior management feel good too. You are perceived as someone who has a positive influence on the organization, someone the organization wants to keep. When you are promoted, you are given another challenging job and the positive cycle continues.

However, that's not all. Because you are deemed important, management is sure to keep you informed. You receive current communication on the state of the company (good and bad), the industry, and the competition. You know about the efforts to improve and impediments to those efforts, and your advice is sought as to how to overcome those barriers. You are also made aware of environmental and personal factors within the company that could be roadblocks to your success.

A. *Position (General)*

Does the position afford interesting and enjoyable work?	1 2 3 4 5
Is the work challenging (will I have to stretch)?	1 2 3 4 5
Will the position make full use of my abilities?	1 2 3 4 5
Will there be freedom to perform?	1 2 3 4 5
Is the position visible enough so my work will be noticed?	1 2 3 4 5

Will the contribution of this position make a
difference to the overall effectiveness of the company?   1 2 3 4 5

B. *Position (Specific)*

Are the responsibilities clear?   1 2 3 4 5

Are the short- and long-term goals of the
position clear?   1 2 3 4 5

Will the necessary authority and resources
be available?   1 2 3 4 5

Are the goals reasonable?   1 2 3 4 5

Who will evaluate me? _____

What is the basis for my evaluation? _____

Will I receive interim feedback (positive
and negative)?   1 2 3 4 5

Do I understand the compensation structure?   1 2 3 4 5

Will I be bonus eligible?   1 2 3 4 5

Are additional incentive compensation
programs offered?   1 2 3 4 5

Are benefit programs competitive (i.e., health,
major medical, dental, life insurance, and retirement)?   1 2 3 4 5

Are there other programs attractive to new employees?   1 2 3 4 5

C. *Unit or Department*

Does my department have influence on
critical decisions?   1 2 3 4 5

Is this subdivision looked at with pride by the rest
of the organization?   1 2 3 4 5

Are management and employees proud to work
in this organization?   1 2 3 4 5

Is there a sense of direction in my functional
area and the company as a whole?   1 2 3 4 5

D. *Communication*

Are the short- and long-term goals of the company
easily obtained and understood by all?   1 2 3 4 5

Is the information I generate communicated and
used by the larger organization?   1 2 3 4 5

Will I be kept informed regarding company
progress (our position versus the competition?)   1 2 3 4 5

Will my advice be sought on critical issues?	1 2 3 4 5
Will I be made aware of environmental and personal factors within the company that could be roadblocks to my success?	1 2 3 4 5

People

The relationship with your boss has long been seen as one of the critical determinants to your success or failure in the job. (Relationships with senior management and others in the organization are also extremely important.) Initially, a sense of security is critical to allow you to learn the things you need to know to ensure success. This can be accomplished if the boss conveys a positive and supportive attitude.

With an initial sense of security, you can approach the things you need to learn about the organization. Knowing the short- and long-term goals of the organization and why they are the goals is important. You need to know what is expected in your job, and you need both freedom and guidance to move forward initially. You also need feedback concerning your personal successes and failures, including suggestions for improvement if necessary.

As you gain experience in the environment, you need an opportunity for greater independence. This effort needs to be conducted in a supportive overall climate, yet it is clearly self-assertive. You need to accept the authority and the responsibility for your work as well as the accountability for what you do. Independence allows stretching and the development of new capabilities and skills. Achieving success through these efforts produces a larger degree of satisfaction from work.

Bosses who can support these transitions are special individuals. They need to be mature, fair, and self-confident. They must understand the need for assistance early in one's tenure with a company and the need to allow independence as soon as possible. They must believe in training and development as a means to growth. It is a great benefit to have a boss who is proud of the number of his subordinates who have been promoted within the organization. Finally, if you can also find a boss who will be your mentor, then you have hit the jackpot.

A. *Boss*

Does the boss have self-confidence?	1 2 3 4 5
Do I sense integrity?	1 2 3 4 5
Does the boss look me in the eye?	1 2 3 4 5
Does the boss enjoy working for the company?	1 2 3 4 5
Does the boss love her work?	1 2 3 4 5

How long does she plan to be in this job? _____

What is her next potential step? _____

Is the boss regarded as a star within the organization? 1 2 3 4 5

Does the boss speak in terms of the successes
of subordinates? 1 2 3 4 5

Does the boss talk about the ever-growing
independence in the position? 1 2 3 4 5

Do performance expectations seem high
but reasonable? 1 2 3 4 5

Are evaluation criteria fair and clear? 1 2 3 4 5

What methods of performance feedback does
the boss use? _____

Does the boss recognize and reward
outstanding work? 1 2 3 4 5

Are training and development important? 1 2 3 4 5

How many of the boss's subordinates have
been promoted? _____

Is the boss proud of the number of promotions
received by her subordinates? 1 2 3 4 5

Did the boss help to prepare those individuals
for promotion? 1 2 3 4 5

Is the boss receptive to new ideas? 1 2 3 4 5

Do I sense the boss might be my mentor? 1 2 3 4 5

B. *Senior Management*

Does senior management speak with pride
about my potential boss's accomplishments? 1 2 3 4 5

Is my potential boss regarded as a key player? 1 2 3 4 5

Do I sense integrity on the part of
senior management? 1 2 3 4 5

Does senior management seem to care
about employees? 1 2 3 4 5

Do I like the senior managers I have met? 1 2 3 4 5

Does the organization promote from within? 1 2 3 4 5

Is there an appropriate career path? 1 2 3 4 5

What promotional opportunities will there be? _____

Does the organization value succession planning? 1 2 3 4 5

C. *Others in the Organization*

Are there good working relationships horizontally and vertically in the organization?	1 2 3 4 5
Do people like one another?	1 2 3 4 5
Is it considered a good place to work?	1 2 3 4 5
Is management held in high regard?	1 2 3 4 5
Does communication flow in both directions?	1 2 3 4 5
Are decisions made at appropriate levels?	1 2 3 4 5

Score

	Unhealthy		*Healthy*
1. Company		1 2 3 4 5	
	Poor Fit		Excellent Fit
2. Position		1 2 3 4 5	
	Poor Fit		Excellent Fit
3. People		1 2 3 4 5	
	Poor Fit		Excellent Fit
Composite Score		1 2 3 4 5	

Summary

The theme of the buy side study can be stated as follows: "As a prospective employee, I have as much responsibility to judge and evaluate my prospective employer as he does to judge and evaluate me. If both the employer and I do our jobs well, we enhance the likelihood of achieving a great match." The areas of focus in the evaluation are:

- *Company:* Will the company be a viable functioning entity in one year, three years, five years?

- *Position:* Will I experience interesting, challenging, and enjoyable work with an opportunity for promotion when it is appropriate?

- *People:* Will my boss and senior management support me and keep me informed, set challenging but attainable goals, give me independence to function, and evaluate me fairly and consistently?

Negotiate the Offer

As the interviewing process winds to a successful end, two things should be occurring simultaneously.

1. The organization is coming to the conclusion that you are the best fit and offers you a position.
2. Your due diligence indicates that the company has all the ingredients that excite and challenge you and provides a forum for you to do your best.

It would be highly unusual to reach this point in a discussion with each side having no prior knowledge of salary expectations. Fairly early in the interview process, an interviewer (usually a screening interviewer) determines that the candidate is within the salary parameters (or close enough) to continue the discussions.

In those early discussions it is important for you to remember that the company hasn't invested much time and probably isn't "in love" with you. Therefore, it isn't in your interest to do any more than is necessary to satisfy the interviewer's minimum need level and get off the topic. A typical dialog might sound like:

INTERVIEWER: What kind of salary package are you looking for?

CANDIDATE: I'd really have to find out more about the job challenge and responsibilities before I could attach a price tag.

If the interviewer is willing to accept this answer, which is basically deferring the discussion, it should be fine with you. At a later date, when the company has "fallen in love" with you, you gain considerably more leverage.

But suppose the previous conversation didn't satisfy the interviewer's minimal information need. The conversation might continue:

INTERVIEWER: How much were you making in your last position?

When the question is worded like this, a specific answer is necessary. It is in your best interest to leave yourself as much flexibility for later negotiations as possible. Suppose your base was $100,000, and over the last five years you received bonuses of $23,000, $15,000, $37,000, $32,000, and $40,000. Then your response might be:

CANDIDATE: My base was $100,000 and my bonus has ranged between $15,000 and $40,000.

At an early stage of the interviewing process this probably meets the interviewer's minimal need, and you should stop there unless you received some unusual form of compensation that significantly added to your compensation (such as stock options). Then you would want to add that information to the discussion. Usually it is not necessary to discuss benefits and other perks at this time.

Once you have outlined your salary range for the interviewer, the next comment or look is a telling one. If the interviewer says, "That's no problem," it presents a completely different picture than if she pales, swallows and says, "That's significantly above our salary range." A third possibility is no response, which is usually an indication that the interviewer has heard you and you are in the ballpark.

If the interviewer indicates that your salary is significantly above the range, you need to find the limits of the range. If there is no possible match, you can save yourself and the company time. You might ask:

CANDIDATE: Can you tell me the range you have in mind for the position?

Usually the interviewer responds to this request because it is not helpful for her to continue the conversation if there is no chance for a match. She might say:

INTERVIEWER: The maximum base we would pay is $90,000 with a 30 percent bonus.

Now the ball is back in your court. In this case your positions are not too far apart, although you would like an increase above your $100,000 base salary. Do you continue the discussions or do you move on to other opportunities? The decision often hinges on a number of issues. For example, is it the screening interviewer or the hiring interviewer who is giving you this information? Remember that a hiring interviewer who is "in

---

INTERVIEW TIP—SALARY DISCUSSION

Try to hold off a discussion of salary for as long as possible. At a later date, when the company has "fallen in love" with you, you gain additional leverage.

---

love" can do a lot of things a screening interviewer never thought possible. Other questions you might consider are:

Is this a company I really want to work for?

Is this the department that drives the business?

The Offer

If you decide to proceed, you may not have to deal with a compensation discussion again until an offer is on the table at the back end of the job search process. Let's suppose that you have just completed your tenth and last interview with the person who will be your direct boss. She tells you that everyone at the company thinks you're terrific and she is offering you the position. She tells you how she went to bat for you and offers you $100,000 with a maximum 30 percent bonus. She also tells you that you are eligible for a strong health benefit package, disability insurance, life insurance, a pension plan, and two weeks vacation. You indicate how excited you are with the offer and how you are looking forward to working for her and the company. You also indicate that you would like to think about the offer for a day or two and you'll be back with your answer. You also ask if your boss would mind if you looked over the benefits manual. She indicates that the vice-president of human resources will be in touch with you.

The next day the vice-president calls you and invites you to come in. While you are performing your due diligence concerning the benefits packages, the vice-president tells you how excited he is that you're considering joining the organization and asks how you're doing. (He is floating a trial balloon.) This is a great opportunity for you to forward your cause. You tell him that you are really excited about the job, company, and people and that you are just wrestling with a couple of issues. When he asks which ones, you indicate that the base is the same as you had previously but the bonus and vacation are less.

The next day you call your potential boss and ask for a face-to-face meeting to discuss a few issues about the position and the compensation. (*Note:*

This meeting must be face-to face. Telephone conversations are unacceptable.) When you arrive at the meeting, you have a cordial greeting and continue additional rapport building. This is another great opportunity and you do not cut off the rapport building. You then discuss the position as you understand it so that you are clear on the goals and objectives for the first six months to one year, job responsibilities, resources, and the means of determining whether you accomplish your goals. You want no surprises. When that conversation is complete, your potential boss may ask if you are ready to accept. The conversation may proceed as follows:

CANDIDATE: There are three issues I'd like to discuss.

INTERVIEWER: What are they?

CANDIDATE: Base salary, bonus, and vacation.

INTERVIEWER: Let's talk about the base salary first.

CANDIDATE: I know you have gone to bat for me over base salary and I greatly appreciate it. My concern is that I have not had an increase in over a year and I do not want to fall behind.

INTERVIEWER: What did you have in mind?

CANDIDATE: I was hoping for a 10 percent or 15 percent increase.

INTERVIEWER: What about bonus?

CANDIDATE: Previously, I had a maximum 40 percent bonus.

INTERVIEWER: Did you receive the maximum each year?

CANDIDATE: No, I didn't, but I received close to it.

It is becoming clear at this point that your potential boss is fact finding. She may or may not give you an answer on the spot.

INTERVIEWER: What is the issue with vacation?

CANDIDATE: I have had four weeks vacation and two weeks seems a bit restrictive.

INTERVIEWER: Are these all of the issues?

CANDIDATE: Yes, they are.

[*Note:* That's it. No more issues can be raised.]

INTERVIEWER: You've raised some tough issues. I'm going to need some time to work on them and I can't promise where they'll come out. As you know we want you to join us and I'll do my best.

CANDIDATE: I really appreciate your help. I want to reiterate how excited I am about working with you.

You have now exhausted your one and only shot at negotiating an offer and now it's time to wait. When the interviewer comes back with the com-

> ### INTERVIEW TIP—FOCUS
> Always talk about what you can do for the company (achieve its goals) before you talk about what the company can do for you (total compensation package including benefits).

pany's final offer, you either accept it and go to work or reject it and move on. Suppose the interviewer calls back with the following news:

> INTERVIEWER: Our best offer is a base salary of $110,000 with a maximum bonus of 35 percent. The bonus is company policy and I can't change that. The vacation is also a matter of policy at two weeks, but if you'll trust me I'll work with you to be sure you get fair vacation time.

Your response might well sound like this:

> CANDIDATE: That's more than fair. I accept and I'm really excited. I want to thank you again for all you've done. I'd like to take about a week to wrap up some personal matters.
> INTERVIEWER: That's fine, except that we have one day of important departmental meetings this Thursday. Is there a chance you could come?
> CANDIDATE: Absolutely. I'll see you Thursday.
> INTERVIEWER: That's great. I'll see you on Thursday morning at 8:00.
> CANDIDATE: I'm looking forward to it.

Midlevel Positions

If your salary is in the midlevel, say $40,000 to $70,000, the approach is the same as in our prior discussion, but you normally have less room to negotiate. Let's say that in your previous job your salary was $45,000, there was no bonus, and you had two weeks' vacation and a benefit package. Suppose the interviewer offered you $47,000, no bonus, and two weeks' vacation. You had hoped for a better package. You would thank the interviewer, tell her how excited you are about the potential of working together, and ask for a day or two to think about the offer and to investigate the benefit package.

When you return to negotiate, you have another opportunity to build rapport and to make sure that you understand all aspects of the position including the job objectives. Then the conversation might proceed as follows:

> INTERVIEWER: Are you prepared to accept our offer?
> CANDIDATE: I'm really excited about the potential of working with you. There are just a few issues I'd like to discuss.

INTERVIEWER: What are they?

CANDIDATE: I thought the benefit package was outstanding, but I'd like to talk about the base salary, bonus, and vacation.

INTERVIEWER: Let's take your questions one at a time.

CANDIDATE: I appreciate the offer of a base salary of $47,000. From my recent study of the marketplace, other firms seemed to be paying somewhat higher.

INTERVIEWER: What did you have in mind?

CANDIDATE: My study found that $52,000 to $55,000 was closer to market value.

INTERVIEWER: What other issues did you have?

CANDIDATE: I wondered whether this position was bonus-eligible and whether there was any flexibility in the two weeks' vacation?

INTERVIEWER: At the current salary, the position is not bonus-eligible and the vacation allocation in this company is strictly according to policy. However, there may be some flexibility and I'm willing to go to bat for you.

CANDIDATE: Thanks so much. I really appreciate that.

As in the previous example, you have taken your one shot at negotiating. When the interviewer comes back with the offer, you either accept it or move on. Let's assume the interviewer comes back with the following:

INTERVIEWER: I'm excited to tell you that I was able to get you a base of $50,000 and at that level there is a maximum 10 percent bonus possibility. The vacation, however, must remain at two weeks for the first three years.

Your response might be:

CANDIDATE: That's wonderful. I accept and I really appreciate your efforts on my behalf. I will work hard as a member of your team.

Recent Graduates

If you are a recent graduate or have only a few years of experience, you may not have the luxury of negotiating an offer. The human resource professional most likely tells you that the salary for entry level associates is x and the benefit package is y. While that may be true, you can still begin the learning process for future moves. Ask him to explain how the salary structure works, what a typical progression might be, at what point someone is eligible for the bonus pool, stock options, and so on. Many young people don't find out about these things because they don't ask.

INTERVIEW TIP—NEGOTIATION

You only get one shot at negotiating an offer. Listen to the total offer, including compensation and noncompensation items, take time to think about the offer, and then, if necessary, come back to negotiate the offer.

As you gain experience (even a few years), negotiating an offer becomes possible, although within a fairly narrow range. All companies do not pay at the same rate, but, when hiring a new employee, most hiring managers like to give an important hire an increase over their previous salary. This opens up possibilities for negotiation. Two important factors are that most positions are covered by two or three different salary ranges and you would like to enter a new position below the 50th percentile of a range because that allows your boss to give you greater salary increases. If the human resource professional indicates that the salary you are discussing is at the high end of the salary range, ask if it is possible to move you to a higher salary range (so that your salary is lower on the new range and presumably below the 50th percentile for that salary range).

Attitude is absolutely critical in negotiating an offer. You should approach it from a win-win perspective where you are attempting to work out a package that is good for you and fair to the company. Anything short of this causes you to be unhappy or causes the company to feel that you robbed them. The response is to exact blood from you in return. It is critical to remain calm, objective, and businesslike. Do your homework before arriving at the negotiation and have your issues written down so that you don't forget them. Ask questions like, "Is it possible to place me in a higher salary range?" rather than, "I need $x." Remember that, when the negotiating is over, you will be working together and you want it to be on the best possible terms.

Summary

Negotiating the offer is an opportunity for the candidate to demonstrate important professional skills, assist the interviewer to create a win-win agreement that will have everyone feeling good, and continue the bonding process. Negotiating skills include:

- Preparation for negotiating.
- Professional demeanor that is objective and businesslike.
- The desire to create a win-win agreement.

Cross the Finish Line

We're at the end of the journey and it's time to recap. Your preparation is complete. Your self-confidence is sky high. You stand at the threshold of the interview and you are ready. You are in outstanding physical shape, ready for one or multiple interviews, and you have full knowledge of your competencies and accomplishments.

As you look forward to the interview, your goals are crystal clear. You engage the interviewer in a challenging, fun, and intellectually stimulating conversation centered on her business goals. Building rapport with the interviewer is of critical importance because this is the basis for her determining that you are the best fit for the company.

As the interviewer makes the transition to the business portion of the interview, you concentrate on helping her to accomplish her agenda (determining whether your personality, training, and skills are right for the position and company). As this goal is accomplished, pockets of opportunity allow you to accomplish your agenda (to understand the interviewer's business goals and to sell your abilities to accomplish them). Since your behavior is proactive, you demonstrate the very initiative and drive that are vital in today's business climate.

While being interviewed, you are conducting your own investigation to decide if this is the right position and company for you, your family, and your career. When the offer comes, you negotiate a fair and equitable compensation package. It takes more, however, than preparation and strategic interviewing skills alone to win the killer interview. It takes passion.

A close friend of ours is getting ready to run her fourth New York City Marathon. It is especially meaningful to her this year since she had serious surgery only five months ago. She has been preparing psychologically for this race for several months, and she is accomplishing rigorous distance training every day to be physically fit. She knows the race course intimately and can picture every punishing hill. She knows what she'll need to do to adjust to the unpredictable New York weather in November.

It is clear that this year's marathon will be a grueling journey for her, but her whole face lights up when she speaks of the finish line.

> To give yourself a meaningful challenge, to commit yourself to a preparation that will place you at the top of your form and then to know with complete certainty that you have the skills and mindset to propel yourself through the inevitable "wall" at the eighteen-mile mark, it's such a high. The feeling of joy at the finish line is indescribable. It's not the crowds cheering or seeing myself on a giant TV screen as I push the final yards. It's the overwhelming personal satisfaction of a quest undertaken and a job well done.

We guarantee that you'll have similar feelings when you cross your own finish line of the interview process. Congratulations on your thorough preparation, on your knowledge of the road and the necessary adjustments, and on your well thought-out acceptance of the job offer. God speed. You'll do well.

Appendix **A**

Key Interview Tips

1. **Scheduling** (p. 49)—Leave plenty of time at both ends of the interview so that you arrive early and can remain late. This reduces stress and shows interest.

2. **Congenial Attitude** (p. 50)—Treat every person you meet as if he were the CEO. He might have a direct connection to the CEO or even be the CEO himself.

3. **Dress** (p. 53)—Your dress should be appropriate and on the conservative side for the company (and industry).

4. **Positive Comments** (p. 66)—Speak only positively about your company (or former company) and the people in the organization—there is no room in an interview for disparaging remarks, however lighthearted their intent.

5. **Preparation** (p. 68)—Be prepared to give examples of your leadership and management abilities in your personal as well as your business life.

6. **Positive Attitude** (p. 72)—Interviewers look for positive, can-do candidates who are self-starters and eager to accept a challenge.

7. **Physical Exercise** (p. 73)—Exercising on the day of the interview enables you to relax and gives you a chance to focus. Exercise 75 to 100 percent of a normal workout.

8. **Professionalism** (p. 73)—Be sure you have all pertinent materials and information, such as extra resumes, research reports, annual reports, and financials. Anticipate having to wait before you are interviewed.

9. **Initial Greeting** (p. 74)—A warm smile and a firm handshake make a strong first impression.

10. **Developing Needs** (p. 79)—Ask what the interviewer's problems are and confirm that you understand them before you tell him how you can help to solve them.

11. **Problem Solving** (p. 82)—You must be willing to take some risks in discussing how you might solve a problem, but you don't want to appear inflexible or dogmatic. You might say, "We've tried X and had some success" or "Have you tried Y?"

12. **Business Examples** (p. 84)—Never tell the interviewer how to "fix" his problem. He may have been trying to fix it for some time without success. Rather, say something like, "I've dealt with problems like that. We have had some success trying a ... b ... c...." Discuss accomplishments.

13. **Eye Contact** (p. 88)—Make eye contact throughout the interview. This is particularly critical when being asked about potential concerns or weaknesses.

14. **Timetable** (p. 90)—Ask about the interviewer's timetable for filling the position. Knowing that enables you to manage the timing of your job campaign effectively.

15. **Answering Questions** (p. 97)—Answer the interviewer's questions directly and concisely. This gives the interviewer confidence that you are willing to help accomplish the agenda.

16. **Business Conversation** (p. 97)—The goal is to create an exciting, stimulating 50–50 percent business conversation throughout the interview.

17. **Relax** (p. 106)—We're serious. Relax! Approach the interview as an enjoyable opportunity.

18. **Bond** (p. 106)—If the interviewer "falls in love" with you, great things can happen. You may be hired, for example. If rapport is not built, nothing good can happen.

19. **Build Rapport** (p. 107)—Don't cut rapport building short. The interviewer does it soon enough.

20. **Length of Answer** (p. 110)—Keep your answers short. No answer should be longer than 60 seconds.

21. **Competencies/Accomplishments** (p. 117)—Present two to four of your strongest competencies and be prepared to defend them by citing bottom-line accomplishments.

22. **Consultation** (p. 118)—Propose how you can help to solve the needs or how the organization can use your skills.

23. **Overcoming Objections** (p. 121)—Resolving a concern gives you a terrific opportunity to clarify something you said, to put forth additional skills, and to extend the interview.

24. **Ask for the Job** (p. 122)—Interviewing is no place for the timid. If you find a job you really want, and if you are qualified and well-prepared enough to get an interview, tell the interviewer you want to work for him.

25. **Salary Discussion** (p. 161)—Try to hold off a discussion of salary for as long as possible. At a later date, when the company has "fallen in love" with you, you gain additional leverage.

26. **Focus** (p. 163)—Always talk about what you can do for the company (achieve its goals) before you talk about what the company can do for you (total compensation package including benefits).

27. **Negotiation** (p. 165)—You only get one shot at negotiating an offer. Listen to the total offer, including compensation and noncompensation items, take time to think about the offer, and then, if necessary, come back to negotiate the offer.

Career Profiles Index

Index

About the Authors

FREDERICK W. BALL is Executive Vice-President of Goodrich & Sherwood Associates, Inc., a New York based human resources consulting firm where he manages executive development and career transition/outplacement divisions. He is a former executive director of a research arm of Columbia University, from which he earned his doctorate degree.

BARBARA B. BALL is president of Ball & Associates, a New Jersey-based communications/human resources consulting practice whose clients include Fortune 100 companies. A school administrator, she is a graduate of Rosemont College (B.A.) and Kean College (M.A.). The Balls live in Westfield, New Jersey.